# THE LEGACY OF
# THE BLESSING

# THE LEGACY OF THE BLESSING
## A Mother's Devotional

Gary Smalley
and John Trent, Ph.D.
*with*
Betsy Lee

**THOMAS NELSON PUBLISHERS**
Nashville

Published in Nashville, Tennessee, by Janet Thoma Books, a division of Thomas Nelson, Inc., and distributed in Canada by Word Communications, Ltd., Richmond, British Columbia, and in the United Kingdom by Word (UK), Ltd., Milton Keynes, England.

Unless otherwise indicated, Scripture quotations are from the NEW KING JAMES VERSION of the Bible. Copyright © 1979, 1980, 1982, Thomas Nelson, Inc., Publishers.

Scripture quotations marked NIV are from The Holy Bible: NEW INTERNATIONAL VERSION. Copyright © 1978 by the New York International Bible Society. Used by permission of Zondervan Bible Publishers.

Scripture quotations marked KJV are from the KING JAMES VERSION.

**Library of Congress Cataloging-in-Publication Data**

Smalley, Gary.
    The legacy of the blessing : a mother's devotional / Gary Smalley, John Trent.
      p.      cm.
    ISBN 0-8407-7791-4
    1. Mothers—Prayer-books and devotions—English.
    2. Devotional calendars.   3. Blessing and cursing.
    I. Trent, John T.   II. Title.
    BV4529.S473   1994
    242'.6431—dc20               93–25521
                                   CIP

Printed in the United States of America
1 2 3 4 5 — 97 96 95 94

# *Introduction*

Several years ago, we wrote a book called *The Blessing*. That book described the deep hunger we all have for acceptance and unconditional love. Since the book was published, we have been flooded with letters and phone calls from men and women who have related tragic stories of what it is like to miss out on their families' blessing. Apparently we struck a heart chord in many people.

Perhaps you grew up in a home apart from the blessing, never really sure of your parents' love and approval. You don't want the same thing to happen to your own children. Or perhaps you were fortunate enough to grow up in a home where you felt loved, but things were different then. The world your children face today is uncertain and sometimes terrifying, tugging at the roots of who they are like a whirlwind. You want them to feel anchored in love and faith.

The premise of *The Blessing* and the premise of this book is that God is the only true Source of Blessing. Receiving His love and acceptance allows us to give that same love and acceptance to others—not only to our children, but also to our husbands, friends, neighbors, everyone we meet.

This devotional begins by focusing on how you as a mom can open yourself to God's blessings. The legacy of God's love is first poured out on us before we can pass it on to others.

The blessing is passed on through five specific elements: 1) meaningful touch, 2) the spoken word, 3) expressing high value, 4) picturing a special future, and 5) active commitment. These powerful relationship elements developed in Old Testament homes can be applied in our modern homes to strengthen family ties.

By looking closely at these principles, you can gain practical skills to become a source of blessing to your children. You can even learn how to reclaim the blessing in your own life if you missed it while growing up.

These same principles can be used to enhance any intimate relationship. A special section focuses on how the elements of the blessing can enrich marriages. Another section suggests how friendships can be deepened by applying these biblical truths.

Beyond the inner circle of your family and friends, the blessing can also be given to neighbors, colleagues, anyone who crosses your path. So this devotional also challenges you to bless others in an ever-widening circle of relationships.

Finally, we focus on how you can grow as a person of blessing and teach your children to become people of blessing.

As you read this devotional, day by day, we pray you will come to see how special and loved you are by your heavenly Father, and how much His love can bless others through you.

# THE LEGACY OF
# THE BLESSING

*The blessing of the LORD makes one rich . . .*
—PROV. 10:22

Think of all the good things you want to bestow on your children. Not just college educations or bank accounts, but values such as love and joy, faith, integrity; that which will equip them to lead happy, whole lives.

How can you give your children this legacy of which love is the greatest?

By entering into a love relationship with the living God, a God who longs to bless you. His desire is to help you experience life at its richest, and to provide unconditional acceptance. He is the Source of blessing. He can empower you to be a blessing to others.

God is the One who first passes on the legacy to us. We, in turn, are gifted to share it with our children, our husbands, our friends.

The blessing begins with you as you learn to receive God's love yourself and then let it flow out to others.

*Oh, Lord, teach me to find my riches in You.*

> *So God created man in His own image; in the*
> *image of God He created him; male and female*
> *He created them. Then God blessed them.*
> —GEN. 1:27–28

Blessing has been in the heart of God since the dawn of time. From the moment He created order out of chaos and light to dispel darkness; from the moment He spoke life into being, His intent was to create something good and wonderful.

His crowning accomplishment was to create human beings "in his own image." God is love. To reflect God's image is to be loving too. When God blessed men and women, He gave them the gift of life. He trusted them to care for each other and all His creation with the same love.

Take a moment to imagine what it would have been like to have been Eve, the first woman, waking up fresh and hopeful. Just as God wanted the best for Eve, He wants the best for you. He blesses who you are: the qualities that make you unique, your hopes and dreams. He blesses what you have to do today, making you productive and giving you joy in those tasks. You are a new creation!

*Heavenly Father, thank You for birthing me in love.*

*And as the bridegroom rejoices over the bride, so
shall your God rejoice over you.*     —ISA. 62:5

Before Denise dashed off in a thousand directions,
she liked to quiet herself by meeting God in the morning. Sometimes she walked to the woods near her
house to experience God's rest and refreshment.

She wanted her two daughters to learn to find peace
in a busy world, also, so she shared this special place
with them. One day she took her twelve-year-old
daughter along the path she walked, to a little hill in
the center of the woods. As they walked along, she
asked her daughter, "Honey, what would Jesus look
like if He were standing on the top of the hill waiting
for us?"

"He'd look happy to see us coming," said her
daughter.

They walked to the top of the hill. Denise said,
"Sometimes I stand here and imagine Jesus looking at
me with great love."

"Just like a bride," her daughter said in awe.

Denise smiled. She was surprised her little girl could
put into words the way the Lord of love made her feel.
But that was it: beloved, cherished, adored . . . like a
bride.

———————

*Lord, help me to drink in Your look of love throughout the day.*

> *God is the strength of my heart.*
> —PS. 73:26

Denise also shared her devotional life with her eight-year-old daughter. "In the morning, when you've gone off to school," she told Kirsten, "I like to walk in the woods to feel close to Jesus. I like to pray there. Sometimes I pray for you."

Kirsten grinned.

"I'm learning that prayer isn't just talking to Jesus. Sometimes it's listening. One day I began walking out of the woods and remembered that I had not taken time to listen so I stopped—right about here."

Denise and Kirsten stopped in the middle of the path. "You know what? I heard the words, 'Stand tall in Jesus.'" Denise explained how she felt the quiet strength of the tall, straight elms towering overhead.

"But, Mom," Kirsten said, "you *are* tall!"

Denise laughed (she was five-foot-ten). "Yes, I know, honey, but sometimes I don't feel tall inside."

In Jesus, Denise was learning she was the daughter of a King, which gave her confidence and strength.

*Thank You, Jesus, that I can stand tall in You.*

*Blessed be the God and Father of our Lord Jesus Christ, who has blessed us with every spiritual blessing in the heavenly places in Christ.*
—EPH. 1:3

When we are adopted into God's family through a personal relationship with Jesus Christ, we are blessed beyond measure. We may have looked for the blessing in other places—a bigger home, a better job, the approval of others—but only Jesus can satisfy our need for acceptance and love.

Paul calls our spiritual blessings in Christ "glorious riches." What are these riches?

First, we are given eternal life, a forever relationship with a loving heavenly Father.

Secondly, our sins are forgiven. Jesus' sacrifice on the cross atoned for our sin, removing the barrier that separates us from God, from others, and from ourselves.

Third, we are given the gift of the Holy Spirit to help us live out a life of love in the world.

Finally, we become part of a spiritual family of believers, brothers and sisters in Christ, who can meet our human needs through the warmth of a caring community.

---

*Thank you, Father, for the gift of Your Son and all the blessings He brings.*

> *Behold what manner of love the Father has bestowed on us, that we should be called children of God!*
>
> —1 JOHN 3:1

Inside every mom, busily tending to the needs of her children, husband, friends, neighbors, and church, is a little girl who is also needy.

God knows that. He knows that even though we offer others a shoulder to cry on, sometimes we need to be comforted. He knows that while we are careful to build our loved ones up, we also need to be affirmed.

And so He comes to us, longing to have an intimate relationship with us as a parent who loves a child. The Bible tells us that when we accept Christ, we receive a spirit of sonship that causes us to cry, "Abba" (Romans 8:15, NIV). The Greek word *abba* is a warm, affectionate term that means "daddy."

Some of us have never experienced the love and affection of nurturing parents. The good news of the gospel is that our heavenly Father can fill the empty cup of our hearts in a supernatural way. He will not only meet our need, but fill our hearts to overflowing.

*Lord, help me to come to You today as a child, with openness and trust.*

*He encircled him . . . He kept him as the apple of His eye.*
                                        —DEUT. 32:10

Do you remember the joy of becoming a new mom? What ecstasy as you first embraced that child and gazed into the wide, quiet eyes that looked up at you. Breathless with the beauty of a little person, you looked at your baby with eyes of love and wanted the very best for that child.

This is how your heavenly Father sees you. God is a doting parent. Each of His children is supremely valued.

The love that your little one saw reflected in your eyes is only a fraction of the immeasurable adoration the heavenly Father feels for us as His children.

Take a moment in prayer to imagine your heavenly Father holding you close like a little child. Relax and rest in His embrace. Look into His eyes and see how much He values you. Listen to Him whisper, "I love you. You are the apple of My eye. How special you are." Let His love fill you up. . . .

*Thank You, Lord, for loving me as You do. I feel treasured, special.*

> *The eternal God is your refuge, and underneath are*
> *the everlasting arms.*                    —DEUT. 33:27

God's sure presence is the source of all blessing. Moses' picture of the heavenly Father holding His children in His arms must have been deeply moving to the Israelites; they had just wandered through the desert for forty years! As they journeyed, God's presence had been constant, undergirding them with love and support.

Life is scary. We need to rest secure in someone's love to feel safe and protected as we brave the perils of living. When parents bring a new baby home from the hospital, say psychologists, a "holding environment" is created by the physical presence of the parents' embrace and loving attention.

We never outgrow that need. One wise mother discovered how she could use the Old Testament picture of God's presence as a symbol of family togetherness and wholeness. "My kids, who are twelve and eight now, still enjoy having the whole family sit together on the couch or climb into our bed to read or swing in the hammock. We think of these special times as resting in the lap of love, God's lap, His arms around us all."

*Lord, help me to remember that no matter what uncertainty I face today, Your loving arms will carry me through.*

*The LORD will guide you continually.*
—ISA. 58:11

Laura lives in a world of darkness, not knowing how to find her way from the bus to the front entrance of the school building. Once inside she is met by the collision of hallway noises. And standing on the stage in a third grade program, Laura knows she could fall if she stepped out too far. Laura could be afraid, but she isn't. She has a guide.

Even before her school bus rounds the corner of the wide parking lot, her guide is waiting at the sidewalk with Laura's cane in hand. Laura confidently steps off the bus and smiles at her guide, who has also become a good friend. She makes her way through the crowded halls, her friend beside her. And when it comes time for the program, Laura knows that watchful hands will keep her safe.

The picture of a blind child stepping out in faith moves us because we have all felt helpless at times. We need the seeing eyes of a Friend who knows our limits and can find a safe path through any situation we face. So the Lord walks close, continually comforting, protecting, guiding.

*Oh Lord, it is so good to know You're near.*

*The Lord is my rock and my fortress and my*
*deliverer; . . . my stronghold.*               —PS. 18:2

The Bible frequently uses word pictures to convey spiritual truths. Word pictures, that reach both the mind and the heart, allow us to experience God's love in a tangible way. Children, who naturally think in pictures, can relate easily to these words—sometimes better than adults!

Charlotte was trying to explain to her four-year-old what the word *stronghold* means in this verse. "When you are in trouble," she told him, "and you want to run to a safe place, you can go to God."

A smile spread across Michael's face. "Like hiding between Daddy's legs."

*Yes, that's it exactly,* thought Charlotte. When Michael was afraid, especially in the presence of strangers, he ran to his father and wrapped both hands around two towering legs, planting himself between them. In the refuge of his father's presence, he felt covered, protected.

Michael's picture not only helped him understand how his heavenly Father could be a refuge, but it also helped Charlotte better understand. Whenever she felt small and afraid, she thought of Michael's picture.

*Heavenly Father, thank You for being my hiding place.*

*And God said to Moses, "I AM WHO I AM."*
—EX. 3:14

God wants to be our source of blessing—our source of comfort, strength, courage, ability, faith—whatever our need is at the moment. How many times have you seen your children struggling with a project too taxing for them and gently said, "Why don't you ask for help?"

No one ever had a bigger task than Moses. God heard the cries of His enslaved people and sent Moses to Egypt to lead them out of bondage. "What!" Moses said, "You want me to confront Pharaoh, the most powerful man in Egypt, and tell him to allow two million people under his thumb to leave the country!

"How am I to explain who sent me?" Moses asks.

"Say that I AM sent you," God answers.

"But I'm not up to the job," Moses protests.

"I know," says God. "But I am and will be with you."

"But I'm not a persuasive speaker," Moses stammers.

"I know that too," says God. "But I am. I will tell you what to say, and I will send Aaron to help you."

---

*Do you have a difficult task today? Are you thinking, "I am not strong enough, capable enough, brave enough, smart enough"? Listen to God's answer, "I am."*

> *For you will nurse and be satisfied at her comforting breasts; you will drink deeply and delight in her overflowing abundance.*
>
> —ISA. 66:11 NIV

The Bible contains rich language describing the feminine attributes of God's parental love as well as His fathering qualities. We are created in God's image, with masculine and feminine characteristics, which together reflect the totality of God's love.

Here God is described as a nursing mother, satisfying a baby's need for food and emotional nourishment. Have you ever seen a more beatific picture than a baby who has just been breast-fed? Relaxed and fulfilled, the satisfied infant melts into his mother's arms, the picture of contentment.

What's in a mother's milk? All the nutrients necessary to sustain life, to prevent infection, to promote health. It's a mysterious process. While Beth was nursing one day, she tried to explain to her four-year-old that everything Mommy ate would turn into food for the baby.

"Will applesauce come out?" asked Jamie. "Will corn come out?" Applesauce and corn were two of Jamie's favorite foods.

"No," Beth said, "milk will come out, but it is a special kind of milk, even more delicious to the baby than applesauce and corn and more nourishing."

*How sweet and satisfying is Your love, O Lord!*

*As one whom his mother comforts, so I will comfort you.*
—ISA. 66:13

In this verse, God is pictured as a mother comforting a child. The image is evocative and tender. While children are small, growing, or even grown, Mother is usually the one they seek for comfort. A toddler scrapes his knee and runs for the shelter of Mom's lap, begging her to kiss his "owie"; a confused adolescent needs a listening ear, he turns to Mom; an adult son far away from home calls Mom for encouragement and lives for her weekly letters, even though he forgets to write.

The need for comfort is often greatest when we experience loss or rejection or when we feel forsaken. That's when a mother's accepting arms mean so much to us. She draws us close, wipes hot tears from our cheeks, and soothes away the hurt. At home in her arms, we feel restored, whole again, at peace.

Is there something troubling you today? Picture yourself as a child swallowed up in God's arms. There may be tears. That's OK. Let them come. Tears are a cleansing, gentle way to let go of pain.

*Lord, hold me.*

*I will extend peace to her like a river, . . .*
—ISA. 66:12

There are times when mothers have no comfort to give. Pam's mother, who had always been the one to comfort her, now lay in a hospital bed full of cancer. When Pam's mother awoke from the revealing surgery, Pam had the difficult task of telling her mom she had six months to live. Pam not only had to contend with the heartache of losing her mother, but she also had to comfort this hurting woman she loved so much.

A close Christian friend called to support Pam. The friend gave these verses, Isaiah 66:12–13, to Pam: "I will extend peace to her like a river . . . as a mother comforts her child, so I will comfort you." Her friend prayed for a river of comfort to flow to Pam's mom and to Pam herself who suddenly found herself in the role of mothering her own mother.

Pam kept repeating those phrases in her mind as she went back to her mom's bedside. She felt incredible peace as she said what she had to say. Then her mother, who was not a Christian, asked Pam to pray for her. "Mom, God wants to extend peace to you like a river." She prayed and God did pour out a river of comfort to these two needy moms.

*When I am fearful today, Lord, let me draw on the inexhaustible blessing of Your peace.*

*The LORD is my shepherd; I shall not want.*
—PS. 23:1

In Psalm 23, David compares God's love for His children to the way a compassionate shepherd cares for his sheep. In a series of moving word pictures, David describes how God meets the needs of every believer.

First, the intimate relationship between the sheep and shepherd is established, suggesting the close bond between Christians and their heavenly Father. The Lord is *my* shepherd. This relationship is a deeply personal one. Once we are drawn into God's family, His flock, we belong to Him. He knows us by name and attends to our every need—even before we ask.

"Your Father knows the things you have need of before you ask Him," said Jesus (Matt. 6:8). One attentive mom thought about this as she stood at her baby's door watching him rouse for his afternoon feeding. She knew from experience that he would rub the sleep from his eyes and cry from hunger. She was so certain of this that she could anticipate it and be there even before her son felt a need to cry. *How much more must the Lord know us!* she thought. *And how much more attentive He must be!*

*Lord, help me to remember today that You are watching over me and You will meet my every need.*

*He makes me to lie down in green pastures;*
*He leads me beside the still waters.*
—PS. 23:2

It is easy in our performance-oriented society to be tempted to do too much. Moms have children to care for, husbands to provide for, houses to keep, employers demanding productivity.

It is good, at times, to put down our shepherd's staff and be a sheep. To allow ourselves to be still and rest in God's provision, to relax and unwind, to feel loved and cared for. Or, like sheep, helpless to meet their own needs, we may have to be made to lie down and rest!

Take a moment to do that. Prayerfully imagine yourself as a sheep, snoozing in a green pasture. Become aware of God's quiet strength and His tender presence nearby. Let Him come close and bless you. His gentle hand may soothe away a hidden hurt or give a reassuring touch that radiates peace.

Gone is the whirlwind . . . blown away like a large, lazy cloud overhead. How wonderful just to relax, to rest content, and feel refreshed.

*Gentle Shepherd, teach me to rest in You.*

*He restores my soul.*
—PS. 23:3

Have you ever felt shattered, absolutely shattered? You feel like crawling in a hole and never coming out again. That's what children do when they are hurting. They find a hiding place.

Cindy noticed that when her second-grader was hurting, she would crawl into a closet or hide under her bed—she did this especially when she felt angry or ashamed. Cindy wanted to help, but Sara's stubborn independence pushed her away.

One day Sara ran into her room sobbing and slid under her bed. Cindy knew better than to force her out of hiding. Praying about what to do, she sensed that she was to walk quietly into her daughter's bedroom, lie down beside her on the floor and not say a word. So that's what she did.

She waited for a while. Gradually, Sara's crying stopped. She began to open up to Cindy and share her hurt. There was a long silence, then Sara said, "Mom, I love you."

Cindy said softly, "I love you too."

That is how the Good Shepherd restores our souls. He comes beside us gently, listening, waiting, slowly winning our trust until we allow Him to put the broken pieces of our lives back together again.

*Lord, forgive me for trying to make it on my own. Help me to turn to You in my weakness and not be afraid to turn to others for support.*

> *Yea, though I walk through the valley of the*
> *shadow of death,*
> *I will fear no evil; for You are with me.* —PS. 23:4

It was a dark time in Marilyn's life. Some days she even wanted to die, the pain was so great. Even though she had been a Christian, Marilyn had never felt the presence of God in a clear way that she could describe. However, as she walked through the bitter days of her divorce, she knew she was being shepherded; that she was not alone, no matter how deep the pain.

One day her son Stephen said, "You know, Mom, the one good thing about this whole mess is that you met your friend Dar."

Marilyn smiled. She was surprised that her son was so aware of how much Dar meant to her. She had found a friend who was willing to walk with her through the tears, affirm her as valuable when she felt worthless, and encourage her when she felt like giving up.

Dar prayed with her and helped her understand the Bible because that was where, she said, the real source of blessing was. But it would take time to clearly claim that for her own. In the meantime, God was shepherding her through Dar. That took the fear away.

---

*You never walk alone.*

*You anoint my head with oil; my cup runs over.*
*Surely goodness and mercy shall follow me all the*
*days of my life.*                              —PS. 23:5–6

David ends his well-loved psalm on a high note of praise. "My cup runs over!" This is exactly what Christ intended when He said He had come that we might have life and have it in abundance. Secure in the hands of a loving Lord, a Christian can enjoy life to the fullest, free of anxiety and fear.

David enjoyed the Lord so much he even danced through the streets of Jerusalem, leaping for joy. During the reign of Saul, the Philistines had captured the ark of God, the symbol of God's covenant with the Israelites. When David became king, the Lord allowed him to retrieve the ark. David led his people back to Jerusalem, with the ark, in a jubilant procession. David's wife Michal saw her husband dancing in the street and was appalled. "How could you make such a fool of yourself!" she chided him. "You are a king, not a servant."

David was unashamed. "It was before the LORD, . . ." he said, ". . . I will celebrate before the LORD" (2 Sam. 6:21 NIV). David's dance was a prayer for praise for God's goodness.

As Christians, we have much to celebrate!

*Lord, give me dancing feet today.*

*Rejoice in the Lord always. Again I will say, rejoice!*
—PHIL. 4:4

Tess didn't care what the neighbors thought. One of her friends whose front window faced the bus stop asked one day what she and her daughter were doing. "It looks like a lot of fun."

At noon every day Tess walked her kindergartner, Kelly, to the corner to wait for the bus. While they were waiting, Tess took her daughter's hands and they danced in a circle. As they danced, they sang a song Kelly had learned in Sunday school, "Rejoice, rejoice, rejoice in the Lord always!" When Kelly was given a small teddy bear, she named him Rejoice. His little paws were easy to hold on to, so the three of them danced together.

Tess liked praise tapes. She sang along when doing the dishes. Then she would sweep Kelly off her feet and they danced around the kitchen. They would giggle and kick up their heels until they were both out of breath. Long after she was too old to dance, Kelly kept her teddy bear, Rejoice. He was a reminder to Kelly and Tess to keep on dancing in their hearts.

*Release my heart, Lord, to celebrate Your goodness.*

*As far as the east is from the west,
so far has He removed our transgressions from us.*
—PS. 103:12

Forgiveness is one the greatest blessings we have in Christ, a precious treasure in the legacy of love.

When people are loving to us, it is easy to love them. But what about those in our lives, even those closest to us, who hurt us? Or others we hurt?

Gail thought about this as she was walking along the ocean on a summer day. The salt air, the breeze smelled so fresh. She looked back over her shoulder at her footprints in the sand. They were disappearing. Again and again, the waves washed over the sand, wiping the beach clean—like marks on a chalkboard completely erased. She seemed to see the word GRACE in twenty-foot letters in the sand.

In living with each other, she reflected, why are we so hard on one another? We fix blame and hold on to hurt, casting it in concrete. Feeling God's cleansing power so freely wash over her that day, Gail wanted to extend it freely to others. To forbear, forgive, let go, and begin again.

*Please, Lord, help me to extend forgiveness to others as You've extended it to me.*

> *And I pray that you . . . may have power to grasp*
> *how wide and long and high and deep is the love*
> *of Christ, and to know this love that surpasses*
> *knowledge—that you may be filled to the measure*
> *of all the fullness of God.* —EPH. 3:17–19 NIV

Have you ever felt so full of love for a sleeping child, as you stroked a soft, pale cheek, that you couldn't contain the love welling up in your heart? Perhaps it spilled over in tears. If so, you know in some small measure how vast and deep is God's love for us.

Imagine the ocean. Massive, weighty, deep. That ocean is like the fullness of God's love. The deepest part of the ocean—the very center and source of that love—is God's heart.

The blessing is an outpouring of God's heart. That's how much love He wants to spill out on us and our families.

Long after the cup of our love runs low, the unlimited resource of God's love keeps on giving. That source of blessing is always available to draw from and it can continually replenish us. In the coming days, we'll learn how we can pour out God's blessing in tangible ways to those who are special to us.

---

*When my cup of love runs low today, Lord, I'll turn to You to fill it.*

*I will make you a great nation; I will bless you . . .*
*and you shall be a blessing.*          —GEN. 12:2

$A$s God is a source of blessing to us, we can be a source of blessing to others. How are these rich spiritual blessings poured out from one person to another?

Originally, God's covenant of blessing passed directly through one family line, from Abraham to Noah, from one generation to the next, until the birth of the Messiah. Because of what Jesus did for all people, anyone can now experience a blessing through God's Son. The blessing can also be passed on to others by introducing them to Christ.

God loomed large in the lives of Old Testament families. Parents had a great yearning to share with their children the blessing they had received. Passing on the blessing became a tradition with five very specific elements, principles that can still bless children today. In fact, we've found in studying the blessing in Scripture that these principles can be applied to enhance any intimate relationship with spouses or friends, as well as with children.

*Lord, teach me to bless as You do.*

*"They are my sons, whom God has given me in this place." And he [Jacob] said, "Please bring them to me, and I will bless them."*
—GEN. 48:9

For sons and daughters in biblical times, receiving a parental blessing was a momentous event. It gave these children a tremendous sense of being highly valued by their families and even pictured a special future for them. At a specific point in their lives, they would clearly hear words of encouragement, love, and acceptance from their parents.

In Old Testament homes, the blessing was a formalized event reserved for a specific occasion. But today parents can decide to build the elements of the blessing into their children's daily lives.

Did you feel loved and accepted as a child? Reflecting on this question, a middle-aged woman said sadly, "My parents were nice people, they must have loved me, but it just didn't come across."

Are you communicating to your children how highly valued they are? Looking closely at the five elements of the blessing, you can gain practical skills to be a source of blessing to your children and even learn how to reclaim the blessing in your own life if you missed out on it while growing up.

---

*Oh, yes, Lord, I want my children to feel loved. Help me to get that message across loud and clear.*

*Then his father Isaac said to him, "Come near now
and kiss me, my son."* —GEN. 27:26

Isaac's invitation to bless Jacob signifies the first important element in bestowing the blessing—meaningful touch. When Jacob kisses and hugs his father, their physical closeness is an expression of the emotional bond between them. This scene is particularly touching because Jacob is not a boy of four, but a man of forty, and he is still encouraged to give his dad a hug and a kiss.

Two generations later, Jacob draws his grandsons close to bless them by laying his hands on their heads (Gen. 48:14).

Meaningful touch can easily be incorporated into our daily lives—hugs of encouragement, holding hands at mealtime prayers, affectionate bedtime backrubs, merely begin the list. There are countless opportunities to draw close through touch.

There are also numerous distractions that lure us away from family closeness: busy schedules, working late, meetings, phone calls. Can any of these be put on hold?

*Lord, help me slow down and draw close to those I love. I need their closeness too.*

> *The LORD God said, "It is not good that man should be alone."*
> —GEN. 2:18

We come into the world longing to be held, to be touched . . . longing to know we are not alone. We are made in God's image with a deep need for relationship. Think of Michelangelo's famous painting of God, the Creator, stretching out His hand and touching Adam's outstretched finger. In that moment, the blessing of life is given and the blessing of relationship: first between God and man, then between man and woman, then parent and child.

This connectedness is communicated by touch. Touch is a bridge of life for human beings: a kiss is a sign of affection, holding hands communicates closeness, a hug offers comfort.

Touch is more than a longing; it is a basic need. In the 1890s, more than half the infants in foundling homes died, during the first year of life, due to lack of holding and touching by concerned caregivers.

It is not surprising then, that meaningful touch is an important element in communicating the blessing— that sense of being unconditionally loved and accepted and highly valued.

---

*Lord, teach me to affirm with my fingertips.*

*Whoever receives one of these little children in My
name receives Me.*                    —MARK 9:37

Long before a newborn can speak, he can eloquently
communicate through a nonverbal language of love—
the language of touch.

Babies draw us close. Everything a baby does en-
gages his mother in a dialogue of silent communication. When his eyes meet hers, he coos with delight.
She smiles back. Softly, he reaches out to touch her
body, her clothing.

And that infantile touch softens us. While Mom
draws close through feeding, Dad's strong, tender
arms make a perfect cradle to rock a fussy infant to
sleep. Picture a new father holding an infant. That res-
olute, responsible look that produces granite-like fea-
tures melts into a gentle smile, sometimes tears, as this
tiny baby draws out his nurturing side.

"Heaven lies about us in our infancy," wrote the English poet William Wordsworth, suggesting that babies
in their innocence and softness come into our lives
bringing with them characteristics of their heavenly
home. Receiving a new baby into your arms, your
heart, really is to receive something divine.

*Lord, help me to be as soft and responsive as a child.*

> *Then they brought young children to Him, that He might touch them; . . . and He took them up in His arms, put His hands on them, and blessed them.*
> —MARK 10:13, 16

One new father loved holding his infant daughter. She would drift off to sleep, lying like a limp rag doll, arms and legs draped over his broad chest. One day she was no longer docile. Slipping out of his arms like a bar of soap, she shot off to explore the world. "When she gets bigger," he sighed, "she won't be able to lie on my stomach. Someday she won't even be huggable!"

Our babies, too soon, become toddlers, gradeschoolers, adolescents. But no matter how old, they still have a deep hunger to know they are unconditionally loved, accepted, and valued. They never outgrow the need for that assurance, and touch remains a powerful way to communicate it.

Jesus knew this. That's why His desire to lay hands on children to bless them is so moving. He wanted to communicate tenderness and love. What better way to do that than by holding them close?

Do children ever become unhuggable? Even though they may appear to shun expressions of physical affection, the need is still there. The blessing of touch can still be given by a warm embrace, a gentle touch on the arm, or sometimes a shoulder to cry on.

---

*Have you hugged your child today?*

*For this reason a man shall leave his father and mother and be joined to his wife, and the two shall become one flesh.*
                                        —MARK 10:7–8

At all stages of our life, we long to feel connected to another human being. The early closeness to our parents gives way to a new need for intimacy. Think of a bride and groom, standing hand in hand before their friends, repeating their vows of lifetime commitment.

Just as babies and mothers feel the need to merge, so do lovers. Remember dating? The warmth of just being close; touching, touching, touching. Your whole body seemed alive to touch!

Intimacy cannot continue to grow and develop without physical closeness. Yet how easily we can "lose touch" as marriage becomes old hat. One of the leading causes of divorce today is "marriage burnout": two partners, working and exhausted at the end of the day, slip into indifference and become strangers living under the same roof.

Marriages need tender loving care, and touch is one the most important ways to nurture that bond. Even small acts of touching can show how much you value your spouse. Offer a hug in the kitchen. Stroke tired shoulders. Walk in the park holding hands.

---

*"I love you"—say it with touch.*

> *Precious in the sight of the LORD*
> *Is the death of His saints.*
> —PS. 116:15

Touch is the first of the five senses to develop, and the last to go. Just as a baby reaches out to be held and craves physical contact, so we, at the end of life, need the security of knowing we are loved. The touch of someone who cares can be our bridge of life.

During Mary Lou's last visit to see Frances, a friend who was dying of cancer, she noticed that Frances couldn't carry on a conversation. But Frances felt Mary Lou's closeness because she kept reaching out to Mary Lou with her hand.

"As an RN, I remember learning how important touch was," said Mary Lou. "I used to see exhausted families visiting the bedside of a dying loved one. They didn't know what to say. We used to tell them, 'You don't have to say anything, just hold her hand.'"

A heart attack survivor said, "I don't know if I would have pulled through if my wife and boys hadn't been there to hold my hand."

_____

*Today I will hold out my hand to someone I love and not wait for crisis to bring us close.*

*But He put them all out, took her by the hand and called, saying, "Little girl, arise."* —LUKE 8:54

Why is touch so important? Aside from the way it blesses us emotionally—with a feeling of being loved and cared for—studies have shown that human touch is life-giving. It significantly contributes to good health.

Some studies show that the touch of another person may calm people by keeping blood pressure and heart rate low, an important part of staying healthy.

A University of Michigan study suggests that people who have close relationships with family and friends actually live longer than loners. These researchers actually call excessive solitude a "major risk factor for health" and say it may be as significant as smoking, high blood pressure, high cholesterol, excess weight, and lack of exercise in shortening people's lives.

As Barbra Streisand sings in the film *Funny Girl*, "People who need people are the luckiest people in the world." And if what these studies show is true, also the healthiest people in the world.

*A hug a day keeps the doctor away!*

> *At Your right hand are pleasures forevermore.*
> —PS. 16:11

Touch is pleasurable. People are so affirmed by touch that even the smallest touch, even by a stranger, creates positive feelings. Researchers at Purdue University asked librarians to lightly brush the hands of some students as they returned their library cards; the other students were not touched. All the students were then asked to complete questionnaires about their experience at the library. Those students who had been touched, without their even being aware of it, reported much more satisfaction with the library and librarians.

There have been many experiments in touch which show that even the briefest touch warms us, probably reminding us of when we were cradled in Mother's arms feeling deeply loved.

If such brief touches can make strangers feel good, why not consciously use touch to bless our family members? A wife can massage her husband's head or shoulders releasing the pent up tensions of the day. One husband loved having the bottoms of his feet tickled. And children love finger games played on their backs at bedtime.

*Oh, what fun fingertips are!*

*Accept one another, then, just as Christ accepted*
*you.*                                    —ROM. 15:7 NIV

What are the other benefits of touch? Touch is one of the most powerful ways to communicate complete acceptance.

Julie was a single mom who had a child out of wedlock. After the joy of having a baby wore off, Julie began to resent her son. She found she couldn't even touch him. There were several reasons for this: guilt from her past; a lack of touch in her own home; and the fact that Jason looked like his father, who had rejected her.

As Jason grew older, he developed problems Julie couldn't ignore. Friends encouraged her to talk to a counselor. Julie began to see how much she had harmed her son by withholding her love from him.

She decided to make a change by hugging her son every day. It wasn't easy at first. The only time she had touched Jason was when she was angry, so when Julie reached out to hug him, he cried and tried to fight his way out of her arms.

But Julie persisted. Gradually, he grew to trust his mom. And finally the day came when he ran into her arms and gave *her* a hug—a gesture of acceptance she needed as much as he did.

*Heavenly Father, give me open arms of acceptance for my loved ones.*

> *. . . And the flesh of the child became warm.*
> —2 KINGS 4:34

Alice was also a mom who found it difficult to express physical affection to her son. She didn't resent her son as Julie did. She loved Jeremy very much. It was just that he was a boy.

Alice had grown up in a family of girls. Her first two children were daughters, and she found it easy to express affection to them. But with Jeremy there had always been a distance. She wanted to communicate closeness, but how?

One day she asked her sister how she had raised her son. "Boys aren't any different than girls," her sister said. "They need to be touched and caressed and kissed good-night." This was a revelation to Alice who thought her son's masculinity would be compromised if she cuddled him. As she started to demonstrate her love in direct, visible ways, Jeremy responded to his mother with greater warmth.

Children—girls *and* boys—need physical affection like thirsty plants need water. It is a clear demonstration of how much they are loved and valued.

---

*Have you hugged your child today?*

*And he will turn the hearts of the fathers to the children, and the hearts of the children to their fathers.*
—MAL. 4:6

When Isaac blessed Jacob, he asked his son to come close and kiss him. In ancient Israel, it was not unusual for men to demonstrate physical affection for one another. In our culture, however, men typically can't do that, which is too bad.

Jeff, a youth pastor performing a wedding ceremony, saw a dramatic example of this. After the bride and groom said their vows, they wanted to show appreciation for their parents. Handing each a bouquet, they hugged and kissed their parents with affection. When the groom reached out to his father to hug him, his father put his hands up, backing off from an open demonstration of affection, as if to say, "No! We're guys."

Jeff was startled by this, and saddened. It reminded him of his own father who was not very "huggy." Knowing how much he missed his father's touch, he decided not to be that way. He took every opportunity to hug his own son and offer high-fives to the teenage boys with whom he worked.

*What can I do to help the men in my family feel more comfortable expressing affection?*

> *Am I my brother's keeper?*
> —GEN. 4:9

It was not unusual for men to express physical affection in ancient Israel, and it is not unusual in many countries today.

When Ed began to cross a South African street and two young men suddenly took hold of his hands, he was taken completely by surprise. Ed was visiting on a mission trip and the men beside him were complete strangers.

He never did find out if these two men did this because he was a foreigner and they thought he needed their help, or because it was customary to do that.

Reflecting on it later, he remembered that they didn't drop his hands as soon as they got across the street. They held on for a minute as they walked down the sidewalk. Shrugging his shoulders and smiling, Ed said, "It was weird, but it felt kinda good." When Ed returned home, he decided he would consciously use touch more often to communicate caring.

---

*It feels good, Lord, when someone cares for me. Show me if I can care for someone else today.*

*For I, the LORD your God, will hold your right hand,*
*saying to you, "Fear not, I will help you."*
—ISA. 41:13

There is something very comforting about holding someone's hand. A two-year-old wanted to walk next door to play at the neighbor's. It was not dark. She could clearly see the way, but she was frightened to go alone. It was only fifty feet, but sometimes the distance seemed like five hundred and threatened to swallow her up.

"That's all right," said her mother, "I'll watch you from the back door and make sure you get there safely."

"No," said the anxious child. "I want someone to come with me."

The mother could not go, but sent her older daughter, who was four. The four-year-old took her sister's hand. Mom smiled as the two of them ventured out confidently, hand in hand. The fear of being alone had gone.

God knows our fears. When we feel very small and afraid—and many situations can make us feel this way—He will be there to comfort and guide.

*Thank You, Lord, that we can walk hand in hand.*

> *I am with you always, . . .*
> —MATT. 28:20

Sandy's four-year-old was going through a period of separation anxiety probably brought on by moving to a new house, a new neighborhood, a new school. One night, when Sandy turned the lights out at bedtime, Samantha insisted that her mom lie in bed with her until she fell asleep.

"But Samantha," said her mom, "you are not alone. Your family is right here in the house with you. Daddy and I are in the next room."

No, she insisted, that was not good enough. Sandy pointed out that when she turned on the cassette tape recorder, Mickey Mouse and Donald Duck would be in the room with her. "You can hear their voices as if they are right here." No.

Then Sandy said, "Jesus is here. He is very close. He is actually in your heart."

"I know that. But I want someone I can feel."

Touch communicates presence. We need God, but as someone has said, sometimes we need "God with skin on."

---

*Lord, help me to be present to my loved ones through touch.*

*He will gather the lambs with His arm, and carry them in His bosom.* —ISA. 40:11

Touch nurtures. Children seem to beg for our attention at bedtime. Is it because we are so preoccupied during the day? Probably the ritual that children insist upon the most is reading a bedtime story. With a loving arm around a little shoulder, Mom or Dad begins to read. The voice of a loving parent is almost a lullaby and the arm a cradle that rocks a cherished son or daughter fast asleep.

The teacher of a third-grade child told his parents that the optimum age for reading is nine; that is, most children can read books themselves by that time.

Why then do children still insist on a book at bedtime long after that? Because the story read is not as important as the reader. Children yearn for emotional nourishment communicated by loving touch. They love to be carried close to their parents' hearts and reading together is a wonderful way to snuggle close.

The next time your little one asks for a book at bedtime, go gladly. Holding him close at bedtime is one of the best ways you can bless your child with touch.

*The next time my child begs for one more book, I'll read him two!*

*Beginning to sink he cried out, saying, "Lord, save me!" And immediately Jesus stretched out His hand and caught him, and said to him, "O you of little faith, why did you doubt?"* —MATT. 14:30–31

Teri had a twelve-year-old daughter who wanted to be snuggled at night. For very small children, the darkness under the bed is a haven for imagined dangers; for adolescents, lying in the dark gives rise to their worst fears.

Teri asked her daughter why a warm body lying close to her at night was so important. "It makes me feel secure," came the answer. Then she changed the subject. "Mom, what was the most embarrassing thing that ever happened to you?" One of the values of this bonding time, Teri came to realize, was the safety her daughter felt to share her deepest feelings.

As a junior-higher, her daughter was full of self-doubt. She needed to be assured that life was OK, she was going to make it.

Teri's presence was an outstretched hand, helping her daughter keep her bearings in the stormy sea of growing up.

*Lord, strengthen me as I lend strength to my children.*

*"Be patient with me," he begged.*
—MATT. 18:26 NIV

Yesterday we read about Teri's twelve-year-old daughter who liked to be snuggled at night. Not all adolescents invite this kind of affection; certainly in front of friends, most shun hugs from Mom and Dad.

To touch or not touch? That is often the question when your children are in junior high or high school. Insecure about who they are at this age, teenagers send mixed messages: "Keep your distance, Mom, I wanna be cool," and at the same time, "Come close, show me you care."

Looking back on his teen years, (Gary's) son, Greg, said on a talk show once, "When I was in junior high, I used to say, 'Dad, I don't want to talk about it, and don't hug me.' Well, I'm glad now that my dad didn't listen to me. What I was really saying was, 'Dad, I do want you to listen to me and I do need you to hug me.'"

How do you show a resistant teen you care? Try non-threatening touch: touching the elbow, patting a shoulder, giving a back rub. Be patient, understanding, and remember he really does need your hugs. Maybe someday he'll thank you!

*Daily, Lord, help me to tell my children through touch, "You're OK. I love you."*

*Be kind to one another, tenderhearted, forgiving
one another, just as God in Christ also forgave you.*
—EPH. 4:32

Touch can be a bridge of compassion to draw loved
ones close—especially when words fail. Have you ever
been at odds with a rebellious child? Proud and willful,
she digs her heels in, refusing to apologize.

"Does it feel good to feel mean inside?" asked a
mother, searching for a key to unlock her daughter's
resistance.

"No," said her daughter, jaw set.

"Do you want to feel that way?"

"I don't care."

Sometimes talking, reasoning is useless.

For a moment the mother was silent, then slowly she
reached out and put her arms around her daughter.
"Sometimes when two people love each other and
they are mad, one of them has to hug the other one
first."

In her mother's arms, the daughter's taut body relaxed and all the tension drained away. The mother
kissed her daughter, holding her close, letting her love
flow into her.

"I love you very much," were the last words the
daughter heard as she drifted off to sleep.

---

*I will be the first to give a hug when it is needed.*

*But while he was still a long way off, his father saw him and was filled with compassion for him; he ran to his son, threw his arms around him and kissed him.*
                                        —LUKE 15:20 NIV

The prodigal son coming home to the waiting arms of a loving father is one of the most moving stories in Scripture. This picture of their joyous reunion suggests that the father could not contain his emotions and didn't want to. With his whole body and soul, he spontaneously expressed complete forgiveness to his wayward son, a rebellious young man who had squandered his part of the family fortune, never letting his parents know where he was—perhaps for years.

Interestingly, this compassionate father never spoke words of forgiveness. He didn't have the vocabulary to express his deep feelings. But in a single gesture, throwing his arms around his son and expressing his love with complete abandon, the son knew beyond a shadow of a doubt that he was forgiven. The distance between them was gone.

This is Jesus' picture of how loved and accepted we are by God: His blessing is always there to claim and reclaim.

-------------------

*Nothing can separate us from the love of God.*

*May the God who gives endurance and*
*encouragement give you a spirit of unity. . . .*
—ROM. 15:5 NIV

Touch unifies. Visit a softball diamond in the spring and watch second-grade girls sitting on the bench, cheering on a teammate. Rocking back and forth, shoulder to shoulder, they shout in unison, hoping for a home run: "Come on, Carrie, you can do it, put a little power to it!"

In sports, high-fives and casual pats on the body encourage team spirit as teammates work toward a common goal. It's not unusual to see professional ball players, after winning a big game, throw their arms around each other, even jump on each other in celebration.

Not just as teams, but also as individuals, people express their togetherness through touch. Friends in grade school develop a repertoire of hand games that require partners to face each other and go through a routine of sychronized clapping. Together they try different challenges: clapping faster, inventing variations on a routine. It is not only fun, but an enjoyable expression of friendship. With each hand touch, an unspoken message is sent, "You're important to me."

*Touch is a tie that binds.*

*Behold, how good and how pleasant it is for*
*brethren to dwell together in unity! . . .*
*For there the Lord commanded the blessing—*
*life forevermore.* —PS. 133:1, 3

The dinner table can be a wonderful place for brothers and sisters, parents, relatives, and friends to "dwell together in unity." Sitting around a common table can be the perfect symbol for the tie that binds. Holding hands in prayer can then be the fleshing out of that picture.

Holding hands is an intimate act and can put some people off, but if done sincerely and with warmth, even guests can quickly feel included in the family circle with a gentle squeeze of the hand.

To do this, one family developed a tradition of the "secret squeeze." Each person around the table held hands with the next. After the blessing was said, hands were squeezed five times. This was a nonverbal secret message that said, "I love you very much!" Guests were delighted to join in when they learned what the tradition meant.

This family found that by affirming one another with touch, disputes that had been brewing dissolved, family members listened more attentively to one another, and visitors felt valued and easily included.

*Oh, Lord, bind us together with love.*

> *I will not forget you. See, I have inscribed you on*
> *the palms of My hands.*                    —ISA. 49:15–16

The symbol of touch is so powerful that even small acts of touch can leave lasting memories. Amy was nine years older than her brother, Steve. She had been elated to have a brother, but Amy was so much older that her mind was soon on other things. When she went off to college, Steve was left behind. After college, Amy lived abroad.

Years later Amy returned to the States to start a family and Steve, now a foreign correspondent, lived abroad. They lived a whole world apart, yet Steve still felt very close to his big sister. Amy's parents encouraged her to write Steve and tell him what she thought of his articles. Amy wondered why her opinion mattered. "He adores you," said her parents.

Amy knew that she had had some impact on her younger brother's life. He was a writer as she was; he lived abroad as she had. But it wasn't until she looked through a family album that she realized how deep their connection was. No matter what their ages or what the occasion, Amy had her hand on Steve's shoulder in every picture. It had left a lasting impression.

---

*Loving touch can span time and distance.*

*Blessed is he who is kind to the needy.*
—PROV. 14:21 NIV

Meaningful touch blesses our relationships. Holding hands with your spouse, ruffling a little one's hair, placing a hand on someone's shoulder—all communicate love and acceptance. To a child starved for affection, these small touches of affirmation are cherished for life.

Knowing that Marilyn Monroe had spent her early years being shuffled from foster home to foster home, a freelance reporter asked. "Did you ever feel loved by any of the foster families with whom you lived?"

"Once," Marilyn answered, "when I was about seven or eight. The woman I was living with was putting on make-up, and I was watching her. She was in a happy mood, so she reached over and patted my cheeks with her rouge puff. For a moment I felt loved by her."

Remembering this event as an adult, Marilyn Monroe had tears in her eyes. This small act of touch, not even done in a conscious way to communicate warmth or caring, deeply moved her. To a little girl with such an insatiable hunger for love even a crumb of affection had great meaning.

*Oh, Father, I pray that my loved ones will not go begging for a touch from me.*

> *Let him go and return to his house, lest he die. . . .*
> —DEUT. 20:5b

Each of us has a unique association with the word *home*. For some, the word evokes images of freshly baked cookies doled out with kisses from a loving parent, evenings cuddled up to a spouse or child in front of the fireplace, back-slapping laughter over a game of Monopoly, or being tightly and tenderly held while sobbing on the front porch.

For others, *home* is empty, devoid of company, care, or communication. No one waits to kiss them hello. There are no loving hugs, only angry slaps and shoves. For these people, the place they live is no home; it is only a place to sleep and bide time.

We can do so much to create a home out of the place we live. Each time you see your child or spouse look for ways to demonstrate meaningful touch. You will create positive associations with *home* that will carry your loved ones through life's difficulties and associations that will always bring them home—a place they are loved.

_____

*Lord, teach me to bring life-giving touch to my family in our home.*

*And God will wipe away every tear from their eyes;
there shall be no more death, nor sorrow, nor
crying; and there shall be no more pain, for the
former things have passed away.*   —REV. 21:4

It had been a difficult day. On the way to her first day
at a new school, Parish slipped on the ice and fell
squarely on her bum in front of all the kids waiting at
the bus stop. She heard their laughter as she ran back
to her house, bruised and demoralized. When she finally got to school, two hours late, she was greeted
with glares and giggles. In the bathroom she overheard two girls criticizing her outdated jeans jacket.
And when she was called on in class her stutter
popped up.

When Jeanette found her daughter that afternoon,
Parish was curled up in the closet holding the family
cat and sobbing. As Parish told her mother each of the
day's tragedies, Jeanette took a tissue and gently, lovingly wiped away the tears from Parish's face. And
with each stroke of her hand Jeanette wiped away the
pain of the event and communicated understanding
and sympathy to her daughter.

Even the smallest acts of touch can communicate a
wealth of care and love.

*Lord, help me to always wipe away the tears of my children just as
You wipe away my tears.*

*Then Jesus put out His hand and touched. . . .*
—MATT. 8:3

Think of the times you've been touched in a meaningful way: as a child nestling in your parent's arms; as someone suffering loss, warmly affirmed by the hug of a loving friend. Add to these human expressions of caring the transcendent love of God, and touch becomes penetrating, powerful, even life-changing.

Christians are the embodiment of Christ. They are His body and presence in the world, literally His eyes and feet and hands; moved by the impulse of His love to recognize human need, to go where the need is and to reach out and touch that need.

Can He use even a mother's hands? Perhaps your hands seem ordinary. They are chapped from washing diapers, dirty from working in a garden, calloused, cracked. Maybe you think they are ugly. Jesus can do extraordinary things with your hands. Stretch out your hands in love and see.

---

*Lord, use my hands today. They're Yours.*

*The LORD is near to those who have a broken heart.*
—PS. 34:18

When people are in pain, they tend to withdraw. They feel nobody can understand their pain and nobody cares. However, there is One who understands and cares.

Something drew Peggy back to church after many years of absence. She was not prepared for the emotions that stirred inside her. As she grappled with how much God loved her, despite her sin, she began to sob uncontrollably. Suddenly a sympathetic hand stretched out and took hold of hers. It was a small, delicate hand and she noticed it belonged to a very petite woman. "How could this tiny woman's hand be so strong?" she wondered.

She realized that the strength she felt in that hand was not the woman's alone. The current of love she felt carried God's strength. The harder Peggy cried, the harder the little woman hung on.

Finally the church service was over. The woman said good-bye and slipped away. God was very real to Peggy that morning, as though He were sitting right next to her, holding her hand. He was.

*Lord, show me if someone needs Your touch today.*

> *And Jesus, moved with compassion, put out His*
> *hand and touched him. . . . Immediately, the*
> *leprosy left him, and he was cleansed.*
> —MARK 1:41–42

Many of the people Jesus reached out to heal were considered outcasts. Untouchables. Jesus' great compassion for those who felt estranged was most clearly demonstrated when He stretched out His hand to touch lepers. In Jesus' day, no one came close to lepers, much less touched them. To the crowds that watched, Jesus' incredible act of touching a leper must have been a more powerful statement than all the sermons He preached.

To be untouchable is to feel unlovable. The lepers Jesus healed ran home rejoicing not only because their physical health had been restored, but also because they would be embraced again by friends and families.

There are times when people close to us can feel like outcasts. A child is rejected by his classmates; a spouse loses his job; a neighbor churns in the wake of divorce.

"The world drew a circle and drew me out," someone said. "God drew a circle and drew me in." We can reach out and draw people back into that circle of love with a gentle touch or hug.

———————

*Reach out and touch someone.*

*The people brought to Jesus all who had various kinds of sickness, and laying his hands on each one, he healed them.*
—LUKE 4:40 NIV

Like the leper we read about yesterday, Dorothy understood the pain of not being touched.

In a college class, Dorothy's professor asked the students to share what they liked about themselves and what they didn't like about themselves.

Dorothy slumped down in her chair, long hair hanging down over her face. When it was her turn to respond, she didn't say anything. The teacher moved his chair close to hers and gently repeated the question. Still silence.

Finally, Dorothy sat up and threw back her hair, revealing a large, red birthmark that covered half her face. "That should show you what I don't like about myself!"

The Christian professor, moved with compassion, leaned over and hugged her, kissing the birthmark on her cheek. "That's OK, Honey," he said, "God and I still think you're beautiful."

Dorothy broke down and cried uncontrollably. "I've wanted so much for someone to hug me and say what you said. My mother won't even touch my face."

This one act of tenderness began to heal a lifetime of loneliness and pain.

*Touch can not only bless, but heal.*

> *A Man of sorrows and acquainted with grief.*
> —ISA. 53:3

Julie could not face Lily so soon after Bob's death. Only last night, they had received news that Bob, a close family friend, had been killed in a head-on collision. Julie went with her parents to take some food over to Lily, Bob's wife, but insisted on staying in the car.

Soon though, Lily came out of the house, smiling, with open arms, wanting to see Julie, who hadn't been home for a while.

Julie's mind was whirling. *What do I do now? What do I say?* But when they came face to face, words didn't seem to matter. She embraced Lily for a few long, slow moments, absolutely still and tender, and told her that she loved her.

Later, in prayer, Julie asked God why she happened to be at her parents' at that painful time. Jesus said, "I thought you wanted to be like Me?"

That *was* true. She had made a commitment to grow in Christ's likeness. "Lily needed me," Jesus intimated. "I wanted to be there, so I sent you."

*Lord, help me to be willing to go beyond my comfort zone—to reach out to others in Your name.*

*The LORD will . . . bless all the work of your hand.*
—DEUT. 28:12

Touch does not have to be heavy to be meaningful. Light touch blesses too. Even the most casual of affirming touches—a hand on a shoulder, a pat on the knee—can clearly communicate love and acceptance.

Maggie's ministry is in her hands. "I'm affectionate by nature," says this warm woman, "but I'm also responsive to Jesus. Jesus touched people and I feel His urge, His prodding at times to put my arms around someone. I feel Jesus is surrounding that person, at that moment, and my arms are the arms He uses.

"Touch is so misused," she says, "that just to experience good touch in a safe, appropriate way blesses people."

Men especially, she feels, are needy of safe, nonsexual touch.

"There is power in the touch of Jesus," Maggie believes. "I'm just a vessel for His love to flow through. He blesses the work of my hands."

*Lord, I commit my hands to You today. Use them to love and affirm people who come across my path.*

> *As the rain comes down, and the snow from*
> *heaven, . . . so shall My word be that goes forth*
> *from My mouth.*
> —ISA. 55:10–11

In order for the blessing to sink deeply into the heart and have full effect, it needs to be communicated verbally, not only by loving touch.

God compares His Word to rain that waters the earth and brings good growth. That is what His word of blessing does in people's lives and that is what blessing words can do in a family. Abraham spoke the blessing to Isaac. Isaac spoke it to his son, Jacob. Jacob spoke it to each of his twelve sons and to two of his grandchildren.

"But my children know I love them," people protest. "My husband knows how I feel about him." Does he? A hardworking husband may receive praise at the office for all he's achieved; he may be respected in the community for his contributions, but does that really affirm him as much as a wife who says, "I love you," just because of who he is?

And our children, so thirsty for affirmation, need desperately to hear words of love and acceptance. We all need to be daily watered with spoken encouragement, praise, and appreciation.

*Help me be free, Lord, in expressing my heart to those I love.*

*There shall be showers of blessing.*
—EZEK. 34:26

Katherine sprinkles words of affection and blessing on her children's hearts every morning before they go to school. She reinforces her loving words with a warm hug. They have come to depend on these important words of affirmation and won't leave home without them. As school buses and car pools wait, Mom gives each child a special blessing.

To Amber, "You are a gift from God, sweet girl. Be a gift to your teacher and your friends in the classroom."

To Greg, who is worried about a test, "Oh, how I love you, Greg. May God bless your mind, help you to think clearly, and give you the skills you need today."

The blessing is given as their mother holds them close or places a loving hand on their heads or cheek. "I want to grab their hearts before they dash out the door," says Katherine. "Significant touch helps focus them and lets them know how important that moment is.

"It must make them feel good, because if I'm not there waiting at the door, I hear them shout, 'I'm leaving, Mom, don't forget to bless me!'"

*How can I bless my children as they start their day today?*

> *Be filled with the Spirit, speaking to one another in*
> *psalms and hymns and spiritual songs, . . .*
> —EPH. 5:18–19

Words of blessing can be sung as well as spoken. Every morning Cindy and I (John) sing a blessing to each of our daughters. The words of the song go like this:

"Good morning, good morning, how are you today? The Lord bless you and keep you throughout the day. We love you, we love you, we love you today. May the Lord bless you, and keep you in every way."

Keri, the older girl, is now old enough to join in when we sing the blessing to her sister, Laura.

Whether you sing them, shout them, scribble them or whisper them, words of blessing let your loved ones know they are treasured.

One mom sends love notes in lunch boxes, complete with illustrations. "You are the sunshine of my life," says a phrase under a picture of a smiling sun. Beside a red flower, another reads, "Roses are red, violets are blue, I could never get along without you."

*Lord, help me to be filled with the Spirit of praise today for my little ones.*

*We will be glad and rejoice in you.*
—SONG 1:4

In the Peterson household, you never know when you will be surprised—surprised by joy.

You might find one of Mom's notes on your door when you come home from school, "I've hidden something in your room." It might be a Hershey's Kiss waiting for you under your pillow. Or, if you like M & M's, they might be scattered all over the floor. Along with the treat, there will always be a secret note from Mom: "I love you! You're special!"

If you are away at college, you may receive a surprise package out of the blue.

Sometimes you'll find a surprise in the pocket of your coat when you dig in to get your mittens out.

An older son going on a business trip found his favorite candy and a note stuffed in a rolled up sock. "I smiled so much when I found that," he told his mom.

"Being a parent is such a privilege," says this happy mom who rejoices in her children. "I love taking every opportunity to bless them."

*Begin a campaign of blessing. Be creative. Have fun!*

> *For I am persuaded that neither death nor life, . . . nor*
> *things present nor things to come, . . . shall be*
> *able to separate us from the love of God. . . .*
> —ROM. 8:38–39

One night when Debra was snuggling her four-year-old, she asked the child a surprising question. "What could you do that would make me *not* love you?"

Katy sucked her thumb, pulled her blanket to her face and gave a big shrug.

"Well," said Debra, "if you made a real mess in your room, do you think that would make me not love you?"

"No," said Katy.

"That's right. How about if you got into Mom's make-up and smeared it all over yourself and the bath-room? Do you think *that* would make me not love you?

Katy pondered for a while, then said, "No."

"You're right."

This conversation went on several nights until Debra asked, "Katy, is there *anything* you could do that would make me not love you?"

Without a moment's hesitation and a big smile, Katy said, "No!"

"You're exactly right, and don't you ever forget it!"[1]

---

*Lord, help me never to cause my children to doubt my love.*

*My people will dwell in a peaceful habitation, in secure dwellings, and in quiet resting places.*
—ISA. 32:18

Our daily lives are not generally filled with blessings. Walking home from school, our children might be bombarded with snowballs and called names they don't deserve. Our husbands fight rush hour traffic to get home for dinner; snarling commuters sometimes curse them, intent on darting ahead of the crowd.

Our families need to come home to a peaceful environment, free of noise, free of clamor, free of anger. Words of blessing can go a long way to create that kind of welcome environment.

In *The Language of Love,* we share one man's description of a peaceful home: "My family is like a soft, overstuffed recliner, complete with every option and extra the manufacturer has made. *Their words are warm and soothing like a heating element;* their hugs like massagers that ease the aches and pains of life. With them around, I can tip way back but never fall to the ground. After spending time in my recliner, I've got the rest and loving support to keep going. My family is like a soft cushion of love."

*Is your family like a soft cushion of love easing the tension of a harried day?*

> *To everything there is a season, a time for every*
> *purpose under heaven: . . . a time to keep silence,*
> *and a time to speak.* —ECCL. 3:1, 7

Everyone wants to come home to a warm welcome: "Hi! I'm glad you're home. How was your day?"

However, many families come home to a silent, empty house. A handwritten note might be left by Mom telling Jill or Glenn to turn the microwave on for dinner. Dad is working late; he'll grab something on the run. To fill the silence, a stereo is flipped on or a TV.

When the family is together, there may still be no interaction. Teenagers retreat to their bedrooms; Dad is absorbed in the newspaper; Mom is on the phone. Parents may genuinely love their children, but as one busy mom said, "Who has time to stop and tell them?"

The absence of affirming words speaks a message too: "You're important, but a thousand other things are more important," or worse, "You're not worth speaking to."

There is a time for speaking words of blessing—anytime, all the time. And there is a purpose—to provide a sense of belonging and appreciation for family members and to weave the fabric of a close family.

---

*Lord, help me make time to bless.*

*Do not withhold good from those to whom it is due,*
*when it is in the power of your hand to do so.*
—PROV. 3:27

What happens if words of blessing are withheld? Researchers studying human communication filmed two scenes: first, a mother and infant actively engaged in a mutual dialogue. The attentive mother laughs, coos, and tickles her baby's belly; in response, the infant smiles and coos back, happy and effusive. Then Mom returns, this time facing her baby, stony-faced, indifferent. The infant looks up at his mother bewildered, frustrated that contact has been cut off. She is silent and looks away. Within seconds this confident, outgoing infant falls apart. He sucks his hand to comfort himself, cries, drools, shakes uncontrollably, his whole body wracked with pain.

This is a dramatic example of how utterly dependent human beings are on loving interaction with others.

What happens if words of blessing are withheld in a home? Like the crying infant, children feel abandoned. Some withdraw. Without a model for open and relaxed communication, they may have trouble all their lives developing intimate relationships. Others become driven, trying to earn coveted words of approval that always remain out of reach.

*Lord, help me to not withhold words of blessing from my loved ones today.*

## March 5 – WINNING WORDS

*How forceful are right words!*
—JOB 6:25

Lois learned how important words of encouragement are by watching a sixth grade volleyball game.

Ever since her children were small, she had watched them play different sports in city leagues. As a parent, she noticed a big difference in the way coaches worked with teams. Building self-esteem had as much to do with creating winning teams as strengthening playing skills.

This really came home to her as she watched her daughter play volleyball one night. Both of the coaches of her daughter's team were highly competitive, but they offered the girls no verbal support. They stood on the sidelines with expressionless faces, not saying a word. Without a clear expression of encouragement from their coaches, the team fell apart. When the ball was dropped, teammates blamed each other. Aggressive players darted in front of other teammates. Weak players stopped trying at all.

Again and again, Lois saw that verbal encouragement often made the difference between winning and losing. In the game of life, there is too much at stake to withhold words of blessing.

*Lord, help me to inspire my family members to do their best with words of encouragement today.*

*Pleasant words are like a honeycomb,*
*sweetness to the soul and health to the bones.*
—PROV. 16:24

How we communicate words of blessing, our tone of voice, the inflection and volume, is as important as the words we use.

Jane asked her six-year-old daughter, Mary, what she thought Jesus' voice sounded like.

"It sounds like singing."

Mary's friend added her thoughts, "It sounds like a lullaby when you're a baby on your mom's knee."

Mary's eyes lit up with recognition. "Yes," she agreed. "It is soothing. It makes you feel calm."

Jane thought about this. She loved her children and wanted her voice to be a blessing to them as well as the words she used, yet often the tone of her voice was harsh, demanding. At times she even screamed at them.

She noticed that this happened particularly when she was under pressure—dashing out the door in a panic, frazzled by an overpacked schedule. She decided to take this as a cue to slow down. She would "waste" an afternoon with her girls, doing nothing: swinging in the backyard, doing puzzles, coloring. As a more relaxed mom, Jane's words became soothing and sweet.

*Slowing down takes time, but it is time well spent.*

*A soft answer turns away wrath.*
—PROV. 15:1a

Children are as sensitive to the volume of our voices as the tone. At four, Ashley understood the meaning of new year's resolutions. She announced hers proudly to Marcia, her mother. "You know what I want for the new year? No more loud talk. It sounds like witch-talk." She looked at her mother and furrowed her brow in anger, "It's like saying, 'Ashley, I don't want you around here anymore.'"

Marcia was shocked. She always thought of herself as pretty soft-spoken, but her daughter didn't think so. Marcia raised her voice occasionally, but she had no idea how destructive it was to Ashley. "Does Daddy do that too?" Marcia asked.

"Yes, when he does it, it's like man witch-talk."

"What kind of talk do you like?"

"I like it when you are nice and calm inside. When I do something wrong, don't yell. Say it in a soft voice, 'Ashley, please don't do that again.'"

After that conversation, Marcia tried to consciously turn down the volume of her voice.

*Softness shows respect.*

*A harsh word stirs up anger.*
—PROV. 15:1b

There is another home in which blessing words are not spoken. It is the home in which words are used to demean and destroy. Instead of hearing compliments that build them up, children in this home are belittled.

These are not always abusive homes. Even well-meaning parents can be careless with words. Mom has had a hard day and looks forward to a relaxing dinner. Just as she sits down to the table, her four-year-old spills her milk. Angry and impatient, Mom shouts, "Can't you do anything right!" A child turns this anger inward: "I am stupid. Mommy hates me."

Sam hands his report card sheepishly to his father. His father, who was always driven by his own father to make good grades, explodes when he sees some low marks, even though there are high marks too. "You'll never amount to anything!" are words that bite deeply into the heart of a boy who yearns to please his father.

How important words are to nurture the soul and foster a healthy sense of self!

*Lord, help me to choose my words carefully today.*

*How long will you torment my soul, and break me
in pieces with words?*
                                                —JOB 19:2

As parents, we must teach our children to weigh their words, and to make the necessary amends when wrong words slip out.

Overtired and in a fit of anger, Amy cursed her father. "I hate you!" She spat at him and lashed out at him with her fists.

After a good sleep, Amy awoke refreshed and sweet. Amy's mom, Carolynn, told her she not only needed to say, I'm sorry to Daddy, but also to tell him she loved him.

She explained. "When you throw mean words at a person it is like throwing rocks. Rocks don't hurt a wall, but they do hurt people. Daddy doesn't cry. He doesn't show pain, but his feelings are hurt. His heart is bleeding inside."

"He isn't really bleeding inside. Is he?"

"Yes," her mother said, "he is. But loving words and hugs and kisses are like medicine flowing over the wounded place. It feels good. And the hurt gets well. But if you forget to say the loving words, the hurt gets deeper and it is harder to make it well."

---

*Words can wound or words can heal.*

*[So he] went to him and bandaged his wounds,*
*pouring on oil and wine.*      —LUKE 10:34

Carolynn was able to tell Amy about the inner pain her father felt when hearing hateful words. Carolynn had hurt him that way too.

Early on in their marriage, Carolynn used to assault Rick with demeaning comments. She didn't know they were hurtful; they just streamed out of her mouth in anger. Their relationship had been a power struggle and Carolynn resorted to using words as weapons.

Once, after Carolynn had apologized for a belittling remark made to Rick in public, he said "I'm tired of your apologies. They make you feel better, but they're like band-aids after you've sliced people up."

God began to show Carolynn how cutting her words were. Could she ever bind up the terrible wounds she had afflicted on Rick? In prayer, she saw Jesus as the good Samaritan pouring oil over a beaten man's open wounds. Jesus invited Carolynn to join Him in restoring her husband.

As Carolynn showed her esteem for Rick with soft, soothing words—telling him she loved him, appreciated him, needed him—it was like fresh oil poured over old wounds.

*Affirming words can turn cursing to blessing.*

> *A wholesome tongue is a tree of life, but*
> *perverseness in it breaks the spirit.* —PROV. 15:4

Humor can be a wonderful way to show affection and tie a close-knit family together, but if pushed to an extreme, humor can also be cutting.

In the *Gift of Honor* we illustrate this by a visit to the Taylors' home. Mary, the oldest daughter in the family, is sensitive about her weight problem. Instead of affirming her as valuable and accepted in spite of that, the family makes the problem worse by telling fat-girl jokes.

One day Mary wore a new red, white, and blue dress for the first time.

"Hey, everybody, did you notice Mary's new dress?" her sister announced at the dinner table. "Mary and I were standing on the corner today, and somebody came up and tried to mail a letter in her." Ha, ha, ha.

Even her parents made fun of Mary. On a trip to the airport, they pulled up to the terminal and a sky cap asked, "Take your bag, mister?"

"No thanks," Mr. Taylor said, "she can walk," Ha, ha, ha.

Our homes should be places of blessing where we build each other up. Can you imagine what a difference affirming words would have made to Mary?

―――――――――

*Lord, help my laughter not be at the expense of anyone else.*

*Death and life are in the power of the tongue.*
—PROV. 18:21

As a little girl, Tammy developed a bad habit of biting her lip. Her mother used shame to try to get her to break the habit. "Tammy, stop biting your lip. Look, everybody," she continued, making sure she had the family's attention, "Tammy is biting her lip *again*."

It never occurred to Tammy's mother to ask her daughter why she might be biting her lip. As a child in an alcoholic home, Tammy discovered later, her habit was probably due to suppressed anxiety.

The words Tammy's mother used were destructive and humiliating. As a child of alcoholic parents herself, she had learned to use demeaning words to control unwanted behavior. Unfortunately, her words had the opposite effect. Tammy's problem got worse, so did her diminished self-esteem.

Instead of becoming an alcoholic, Tammy became a workaholic. Her compulsive drive to succeed was eating away at her inner sense of well-being until someone introduced her to a heavenly Father who loved her and spoke words of affirmation into her heart. Positive words. Encouraging words. Words that ultimately transformed her.

---

*Do my words bless or diminish?*

*A word spoken in due season, how good it is!*
—PROV. 15:23

Alison held her award for best gymnast in the state. What was the secret of this determined twelve-year-old's success? Good coaching certainly was important, and of course she had put in many hours of training. However, there was one additional factor which gave her an edge: inner confidence, something her mom inspired in her.

Whenever Alison felt anything was too tough—wrestling with her math homework or mastering a new gymnastics move—her mom wouldn't let her throw in the towel with the complaint, "I can't do it."

"Don't ever limit yourself," Nancy would tell her daughter, encouraging her to try harder.

Nancy always wished she had received that kind of support when she was growing up. When she had come home with a report card of A's and B's, her dad would sigh, "Yeah, but you get a F in housework." When she wanted to go to college, her dad thought it was a waste of time. Nancy got a full scholarship anyway and put herself through school.

Nancy could not change the past, but she could spur her daughter on to success with words of encouragement she had come to value.

*Lord, make me mindful of the priceless value of affirmation.*

*Encourage one another daily.*
—HEB. 3:13 NIV

Everyone needs to hear words of encouragement—husbands and wives, as well as children. In *The Language of Love*, we share this word picture of a discouraged husband: "I know I can be a roaring flame of enthusiasm, but my wife often hoses me off with words, and I wind up a dying ember. If she would only fan the fire with some encouraging words or a tender hug when I get home from work, I'd burn as brightly as ever."

This is probably a husband whose ideas about adventurous vacations are met with resistance, "Oh, we could *never* do that." Or a husband whose attempts to fix up the house are met with criticism instead of appreciation, "You make such a mess! Can't you clean up after yourself!"

Can you sense what a difference warm words would mean to this man? What a difference they would make to this marriage? Most parents seem to be aware of how damaging negative words can be to their children, but we forget that inside a grown adult is a tender heart, just as vulnerable to hurt, just as responsive to affirmation.

*Lord, help my words to fan the flame of my husband's self-esteem, not dampen his dreams.*

*Let the word of Christ dwell in you richly.*
—COL. 3:16

Where do we get words of blessing? We can search for words of our own or borrow them from someone else by sending a greeting card. But please, don't overlook the richest source of blessing words—the Bible.

For days after receiving her new Bible at church, Jackie carried it tucked carefully under her arm. "I know why the pages are gold," the second grader told her mom, "it contains all the wealth in the world."

How right Jackie was. The Bible is unlike any other book. The Word of God is "quick and powerful," says Paul (Heb. 4:12). The Greek word for *quick* means "alive" and the Greek word for *powerful* is "energes" or "energetic." The words of Scripture are vital and dynamic, life-changing.

To be a Christian and not open the Bible is to try to nickel and dime your way through life, while never drawing on the lavish bank account, provided by a loving heavenly Father, right at your fingertips. During the next few days, we'll learn how to use the rich resource of the Bible to bless those we love.

*Lord, teach me to use the Bible as a blessing tool.*

*I have loved you with an everlasting love; therefore
with lovingkindness I have drawn you.*
—JER. 31:3

Before we explore the power of God's Word to bless
others, let's first savor the sweetness of the words He
addressed to us.

God longs to communicate His love to us in ways we
can understand. For example, these words were spoken by God, through the prophet Jeremiah, to His people calling them back to faithfulness. They suggest
a bridegroom wooing his beloved. What woman
wouldn't want to think of herself as desirable, as beloved!

Think of the Bible as a love letter. Do you remember
receiving a love letter when you were engaged or dating someone special? Did you read the letter quickly
and throw it away? Probably not. You read it again and
again, drinking in every word and phrase with great
delight, even committing some of it to memory.

Try reading the Bible like a love letter addressed to
you, personally. "I have loved you with an everlasting
love, (insert your name); therefore, with loving-
kindness I have drawn you."

Let those tender words linger with you throughout
the day and bless you.

*Oh Lord, may I hear You calling me to Yourself with words of love.*

> *Therefore you shall lay up these words of mine in your heart . . . they shall be as frontlets between your eyes.*
> —DEUT. 11:18

To store away God's words in our hearts, it is helpful to put them right in front of our eyes where we can see them often.

Marliss was facing some difficult decisions. As a constant encouragement, she taped a personalized verse to the steering wheel of her car. "And my God shall supply all your need, Marliss, according to His riches in glory by Christ Jesus" (Phil. 4:19). Every time she thought about her problems, she looked down at that verse and felt uplifted.

During the course of a month she went from a feeling of hopelessness and desperation to exhilaration as God did indeed supply all her needs.

As she was telling this story to a friend in a restaurant, a stranger overheard their conversation and confided that he was facing some overwhelming problems. Marliss sensed that he needed something to hold on to as she had. She slipped out to her car, took the verse off the steering wheel and gave it to him. She waved goodbye as he drove off smiling, a Bible verse taped to his steering wheel.

*God's Word works!*

*And do not be conformed to this world, but be*
*transformed by the renewing of your mind.*
—ROM. 12:2

An advertising adage states that if a consumer sees a message once or twice, he will probably not notice it. After seeing it three times, it begins to sink in and may motivate him to buy. Consequently, advertisers constantly bombard us with messages, trying to mold our attitudes.

Being transformed by God's thinking rather than conforming to worldly attitudes is a battle of the mind—a battle that many of us are losing! Once you realize it's a battle, you can take steps to stand firm in the Word.

To keep her eyes fixed on God, one woman meditates on Bible verses (written on small cards) as she exercises. Another woman has a refrigerator magnet that says, "Taste and see that the Lord is good," which she enjoys thinking about as she fixes dinner for her family. Still another has, pasted up near her bed, a blessing verse that she prays for her husband.

*Lord, help me to keep Your words of blessing in the forefront of my mind.*

> *And you shall write them on the doorposts of your*
> *house and on your gates.*                              —DEUT. 11:20

Just as we can keep our minds focused on God's Word by meditating on Bible verses, our children can also renew their minds by daily seeing words of Scripture in familiar surroundings.

For children, words are more appealing and meaningful if combined with a picture and tied to their natural interests.

Nine-year-old Anne-Marie loved kittens. On the door of her bedroom (the gate of her house), she had taped up a poster with two furry kittens snuggling next to each other. Under the picture were the words, "A friend loves at all times" (Prov. 17:17).

Thirteen-year-old Tanya loved horses. She had wall-papered her bedroom with horse pictures and had a shelf full of model horses. However, she also wanted to find creative ways to put Bible verses on her wall! When her mom found a calendar of horse photos, Tanya was very excited. Under a striking, color photograph of horses galloping across a green pasture were the words, "Let the beauty of the LORD . . . be upon us" (Ps. 90:17).

*Thank You, Jesus, that my children's minds can soak up the beauty of Your Word.*

*You shall teach them to your children, speaking of them when you sit in your house, when you walk by the way, when you lie down, and when you rise up.*
—DEUT. 11:19

We are instructed to talk with our children, during the course of everyday living, about God's love and the importance of His commands.

Jerry, who was proud of his developing reading skills, always begged to read a verse from the "Bread of Life" box at the dinner table. One night he read, "Be holy for I am holy" (1 Peter 1:16). A lively discussion followed.

"I betcha a million dollars," said Jerry, "that Jesus lost it once in a while."

"Well," Jerry's parents said, "Jesus is the Son of God and *is* perfect. But He doesn't expect you to be perfect, just shoot for the mark of goodness."

Then Jerry said, "Remember when Angie was little, Dad, and you were going to spank her? She said if she were an angel, she could fly over your head and you couldn't catch her. You said, if she were an angel, you wouldn't have to spank her!" Recalling that incident made everybody laugh.

Families need to be at home in Scripture, exploring its meaning together, applying it to their daily lives, making it come alive.

*Lord, You are the living Word. Infuse our lives with warmth.*

> *For the word of God is living and powerful, . . .*
> *piercing even to the division of soul and spirit, . . .*
> *and is a discerner of the thoughts and intents of*
> *the heart.*
> —HEB. 4:12

God's Word releases blessing. But often before it can do that, the Holy Spirit has to do internal surgery to cut away any blockages that obstruct the free flow of that blessing.

Marion wanted to bless her husband. The Lord led her to pray Ephesians 3:14–19 asking that Rich would know the width and length and depth and height of God's love and be filled with all the fullness of God. She was to pray this not once or twice, but one time each day for a whole year!

The Apostle Paul had prayed this prayer for the Ephesians on his knees, so Marion felt she should do this too. It wasn't easy. Exhausted at the end of the day, she didn't feel like kneeling beside her bed on a hard wood floor some nights to pray. But she kept her commitment.

Every time Marion prayed, God showed her something new about her relationship with Rich. One time she prayed without thinking, "May Rich be filled with all the fullness of Marion." Suddenly she realized she was trying to fill Rich with herself! In a year, Marion learned a lot about her true heart and how she could bless more freely.

*Blessing another can be a humbling experience.*

*We do not know what we should pray for . . . , but
the Spirit Himself makes intercession for us. . . .
according to the will of God.*   —ROM. 8:26–27

Have you ever felt at a loss to know how to pray? If
you long to bless someone, God undoubtedly put that
longing in your heart and He will give you the words
to pray. How? The Holy Spirit can lead you to particular words in the Bible that will come alive and speak
directly to your situation.

Fay had prayed for many years that her mother- and
father-in-law would come to know Jesus. One time before she went to visit them a few words from the Bible
jumped out at her and she felt she should pray those
words specifically for them. So she prayed from Psalm
147:18, "Lord, send forth Your Word and melt their
hearts."

She prayed this in faith, but rationally Fay thought
it was absurd. How could God send ahead His Word
into *their* home? There had never been a Bible in her
in-laws' house. During her visit, Fay was surprised
when her mother-in-law asked what John 3:16 meant.
An avid sports fan, she loved to watch TV football. At
every game a big banner appeared on the fifty-yard
line with "John 3:16" on it. Fay was astonished. She
never imagined that God's Word would come into a
home that way!

*God's Word adds power to prayer!*

*He calms the storm, so that its waves are still.*
—PS. 107:29

Emmy sobbed into the phone. She was scared. She had called her friend Diane, hoping for some help.

Diane listened. Tomorrow, Emmy said, she was going in for a biopsy on her breast. A lump had been discovered. Could it be cancer? She was a little ashamed to be so shaken. She shouldn't assume the worst. But the fear somehow terrorized her, ripping away her security and reminding her of past pains. She felt overwhelmed.

Diane sensed that Emmy needed to feel Jesus' calming presence. Just as the anxious disciples on a storm-tossed sea had cried out for Jesus to save them, Emmy needed Jesus to calm the terrible tempest churning in her heart. Words of Scripture can come alive in a time of need. In prayer, Diane pictured Emmy in that biblical story. "Be still!" Jesus spoke a word of peace.

"Thank you so much for your prayer," Emmy wrote in a note two days later. "Jesus is calming the wind and the storm. With His comforting arm around me and His arm stretched out to quiet the squall, only a loving breeze whispers around me."

*When I am anxious today, Lord, I will feel You near, speaking a word of peace.*

*For the LORD will comfort Zion, He will comfort all her waste places; He will make her wilderness like Eden, . . . joy and gladness will be found in it, thanksgiving and the voice of melody.*

—ISA. 51:3

Sherry was going through a difficult time. She wanted to tell someone about it, but couldn't. On Sunday she confided to a friend only that she was hurting. Her friend didn't pry. She simply gave her an understanding hug.

A couple of weeks later, Sherry got a card from her friend. "As I was praying this morning, God gave me this promise for you." It was the joyous verse in Isaiah.

He will comfort all her waste places. Sherry did have waste places in her heart, barren places that felt dry and devastated, places that no one in the world but God could comfort.

Thanksgiving and the voice of melody. Would her heart sing again? Would this sadness pass? Would she again sing a song to someone else?

Two years later, Sherry still had her friend's card as a keepsake in her Bible. It had given her hope. It had been the lifeline she'd needed to pull through her crisis. She had passed on those words of hope to others many times since.

---

*God's Word can light the depths of our heart with blessing.*

> *But only speak a word, and my servant will*
> *be healed.*
> —MATT. 8:8

Can God's Word heal? Watching her six-year-old nephew play baseball, Renee would unequivocally say yes. When Andrew was a year old, she had helped pray him through extensive open heart surgery.

Before the surgery, Andrew's mom, Cynthia, had called Renee for support. Renee prayed with her sister over the phone and continued to pray throughout the day.

Renee wondered how she should pray. "Create in Andrew a clean heart" (Ps. 51:10). Those words kept going through her mind. A clean heart? It sounded crazy, but that is what she prayed.

After eight hours, Cynthia called to say the surgery had gone well. She explained how the surgeon had reconstructed Andrew's heart because a misdirected aorta recirculated dirty (unoxygenated) blood back into his heart, which had nearly killed him.

Renee was amazed. "You mean, they had to create in Andrew a *clean* heart?"

"Yes, I guess you could say that."

The words Renee had prayed described exactly what had been done to heal Andrew's heart.

*How exciting it is, Lord, to be a partner with You in prayer.*

*The LORD bless you and keep you; the LORD make
His face shine upon you, and be gracious to you;
. . . and give you peace.* —NUM. 6:24–26

This benediction is used in many churches to bless congregations as they are dismissed after Sunday service. One church adds a special gesture. At the end of its service, the large Bible on the pulpit is carried down the center aisle of the sanctuary, after the benediction is spoken—a symbol of God's Word and blessing being carried out into the world.

God's blessing is meant to spill out into the world, to bring healing and hope to all people who hunger for acceptance and love.

Once, when facing a hungry crowd of five thousand people, Jesus asked for what food was at hand. Just a small boy's lunch, five loaves and two fish. Jesus held up these meager resources to heaven and blessed them. Miraculously, they were multiplied to feed thousands with twelve basketfuls left over!

Jesus called Himself the Bread of Life. Just as He then fed hungry stomachs with bread and fish, He still feeds hungry hearts with words of love. As Christians, we have the life of Christ within us. Let's share it!

*Oh, Lord, I've feasted on Your Word. Forgive me for forgetting the world is hungry too.*

> *Those who are well have no need of a*
> *physician. . . . I did not come to call the*
> *righteous, but sinners, to repentance.*
> —MATT. 9:12–13

Phyllis was a photographer. Soon she would see her father and give him the gift she'd put together for him; a collage of photos she'd taken of him and his grand-daughters in the apple orchard that spring. She smiled, knowing he would be pleased.

When she looked at the pictures of her family, she had a bittersweet feeling. As wonderful as her parents were, she had begun to see that they had faults and had failed her in some ways. At the same time, she realized that she and her husband, despite their best efforts, would also fail, and even hurt, their two beautiful daughters whom they loved so much.

It was hard to face that fact squarely, which made Phyllis realize that she spent a lot of emotional energy covering up faults—her own and other people's.

*If we were perfect,* she thought, *we wouldn't need Jesus.* Confessing her own brokenness, Phyllis began a journey toward healing and a fuller understanding of God's blessing.

*Oh, Jesus, how needy we are, and how grateful that You've come to heal.*

*He blessed each one according to his own blessing.*
—GEN. 49:28

The heart of the blessing is expressing high value to our loved ones. Meaningful touch communicates the blessing. Spoken words let the message be known. The third element of the blessing, expressing high value, is what our words say.

When Jacob blessed his twelve sons, he used a word picture that depicted how much he appreciated their special qualities:

> Judah is a lion's whelp; . . . and as a lion, who shall rouse him?
>
> Naphtali is a deer let loose; he uses beautiful words.
>
> Joseph is a fruitful bough, a fruitful bough by a well. (Gen. 49:9, 21–22)

Judah was pictured as a lion, a symbol of strength, which reflected his leadership qualities. Naphtali, the graceful deer, was appreciated for his artistic qualities. Joseph, like a fruitful tree, prospered through his love for God.

By affirming each son's best traits, Jacob said, "You're unique and highly valued."

*Lord, help me to look for ways to affirm my children's special qualities.*

> *The Son of Man did not come to be served, but to serve.*
> —MATT. 20:28

Throughout the Gospels, we see Jesus serving, rather than being served: stooping to touch and heal a beggar, reaching down to bless little children, kneeling to wash His disciples' feet.

Honoring others. In Hebrew, the word *bless* literally means "to bow the knee." To show reverence and honor to an important person.

Jesus' example offers insight into how we can bless our children. As parents it is easy to tower over them, not only physically, but emotionally, imposing our demands from the top down.

One mother discovered this when she asked her preschooler to clean her room. She came back ten minutes later and found her daughter playing, oblivious to the litter of toys, crayons, and coloring books around her. This happened often. The exasperated mom soon found herself shouting.

One day she decided to take a different approach. Instead of leaving the little girl to clean her room on her own, Mom got down on her knees and helped—as a companion, not a commander. The work was done much faster and with much less tension.

*Teach me to motivate my children with love, rather than coercion, Lord.*

*Whoever receives this little child in My name receives Me. . . . For he who is least among you all will be great.*

*—LUKE 9:48*

How easy it is to open our arms to a smiling baby—especially a Gerber baby with golden curls and a dimpled chin, the picture of perfection. But what if our children are less than perfect?

No birth announcements were sent out in the Hussein household when their baby was born. The Hussein children were beautiful, brilliant, and accomplished. When one of their daughters had a baby with Down's syndrome, It was viewed as a tragedy. In their home country, handicapped people were publicly ridiculed; sometimes handicapped children were even left in the desert to die. The Husseins were devastated.

By contrast, Jennifer and Rick were delighted to have a new son, even though Seth had Down's syndrome. "We hold Seth and feel the warmth and depth of our love for him," they said in a family letter. "We watch him smile as he discovers his world. It is love that keeps us focused on the blessing of his life."

These proud parents were committed to helping their son be all he could be. They were already talking about the day he'd stand in the winner's circle at the Special Olympics.

---

*Lord, may Your love keep me focused on the blessing of my child's life.*

> *Be devoted to one another in brotherly love.*
> —ROM. 12:9 NIV

It is obvious, to anyone who sees Leah and Seth together, that Leah is devoted to her younger brother, Seth. From the moment Leah's parents brought him home from the hospital, it was clear that they esteemed their second child, who had Down's syndrome, just as highly as they did their first, a normal little girl. Leah, a warm, affectionate three-year-old, was delighted to be on the "blessing team" with Mom and Dad.

"Seth is easy to love," says their mom "and Leah does lots of it. She offers lots of help and plays with Seth when he wants attention. His eyes light up with pleasure whenever she is around and watching the two of them interact is great fun. Sometimes we wish they could both remain children to avoid the difficult times that Seth's Down's syndrome will bring for both of them. It seems, though, that the love they already share will not only get them through, but will strengthen their personalities as well."

Are your children devoted to one another? As we learn to bless our children, we need to teach them to value each other, too.

*How can I encourage my children to bless each other today?*

*We have different gifts, according to the grace given us.*
　　　　　　　　　　　　　　　—ROM. 12:6 NIV

Sibling rivalry ranks high on the list of challenges that frustrate parents. Ron and Debbie tried everything they could to convince their two daughters that, even though they were not created equal, they were certainly treasured equally.

Both girls were highly valued. But as the girls grew older, the differences between them became more noticeable.

One day Kelsie sighed wistfully, annoyed that her sister was doing better in school than she was. "Mom, why did Krista get all the brains?"

Her mother smiled. "She doesn't have all the brains, honey. She has a different kind of brains than you do. That's all."

Debbie tried to explain the difference between Kelsie's creative mind, fluid and artistic, and Krista's analytical mind that made her excel in math and science. Then Debbie asked, "Why do you think God doesn't give one person all the brains?"

"So we can help each other?"

"Exactly."

_____

*Thank You, Heavenly Father, for gifting each of us in different ways and making us incomplete on our own.*

> *Let the little children come to Me, and do not forbid them; for of such is the kingdom of God.*
> —MARK 10:14

Children are important people. Jesus esteemed them highly. He took time out from a busy itinerary to hold and bless them—despite His disciples' protest that He had more important things to do. When our children ask to come to us, what is our response?

Children often ask for attention at inconvenient times. Their agendas very rarely blend with our own. But when we do stop, truly stop, and give them our full, undivided attention, they have the ability to rescue us from our busyness and teach us what matters most.

One busy mom decided to accept her three-year-old's invitation to a tea party. It was not easy to still the running clock in her mind, but soon she was fascinated, watching Kari prepare an elaborate place setting of plastic cups and saucers. As she accepted her tea cup from a dimpled, little hand, the thought dropped into this mom's mind, *This is heaven. What more do you want?*

She had never been happier than she was at that moment, sitting cross-legged on the floor, being treated like a queen by a precious little princess.

*Take time to enjoy your children. You both will be blessed.*

*Let your gentleness be evident to all.*
—PHIL. 4:5 NIV

How gentle are you with your children? Does your tone of voice reflect how much you value them? Do you touch them and tell them how special they are to you? Do you respond with tenderness to them when they're hurting?

If you had a priceless antique vase in your living room, you probably would not shake it around. The value you attached to it would check your behavior. The same thing should be true of your living treasures.

How we treat our children tells them how much we value them. Here are some actions that express tender loving care:

- Gently admit to your children when you know you've wronged them. (This goes a long way toward building their self-worth.)

- Watch or, if necessary, soften, your tone of voice when they make a mistake.

- Listen carefully, don't lecture.

- Cry with them over their hurts. Children will leave home feeling valuable if treated with tender care. And they'll treat others with the same value they've been shown.

------

*Lord, help me to show my children how special they are by treating them with gentleness.*

> *You shall be a special treasure to Me.*
> —EX. 19:5

We are priceless treasures to God—and He treats us as such. Just so should we treat our children. But not all parents do.

Jimmy's parents lived in a house filled with antiques and art treasures that Jimmy could not touch. After repeated lectures and spankings, nine-year-old Jimmy got better about staying away from the costly treasures. He was becoming withdrawn and tense, but at least he was showing respect for his parents' precious possessions. Until one tragic day.

One afternoon Jimmy's parents left him at home while they went shopping. They returned to a shocking sight. Little Jimmy had gone through every room in the house, systematically smashing every precious item he could get his hands on.

Every day he had walked among vases and pictures that seemed to mock him: "We're more valuable than you are. We're handled more gently than you!" That knowledge had simmered within him until his anger exploded.

Do you have things that your children see you polishing, caring for, playing with, or spending time with that appear to be more valuable than they are?

*Oh, heavenly Father, forgive me for not treasuring my children as I should.*

*Let each esteem others better than himself.*
—PHIL. 2:3

It was a sight that would cause most people to stop and stare: a three-year-old and a ninety-one-year-old playing on a seesaw, laughing, and having the time of their lives. There were no two people who esteemed each other more highly.

Carrie adored Great-grandma, and Great-grandma showered Carrie with affection. If Carrie wanted to play Candyland, Great-grandma would play for hours; if Carrie wanted to dig in the sand on the beach, Great-grandma would get down on her hands and knees and help shovel. As the older woman stooped to honor little Carrie, Carrie, in turn, lifted her great-grandma high in admiration.

Though separated by many miles they kept each other close through letters. As Great-grandma went blind, she wrote: "Dear Carrie, I can hardly believe you are going to school, learning to read and write. I'm learning to write, too, without seeing what I write and I have cassette tapes that read books to me."

Carrie's great-grandma lived to be ninety-five. It seemed as if she lived that long just for Carrie.

*How much we have to give each other!*

> *Each member belongs to all the others.*
> —ROM. 12:5 NIV

In order to feel valued and important, children need to experience a strong sense of belonging. Judy grew up in a home that showed little love and acceptance. As the youngest child of six, she was teased by her brothers and sisters, who liked to tell the neighborhood children that her parents had found Judy in a vacant lot—and were ready to send her back!

In spite of this, Judy felt special and valuable. Why? Because even though she didn't gain a sense of belonging in her home, she had loving grandparents who provided the acceptance she needed. Judy's grandparents lived just a few doors down from her house. Judy would run into their home for a snack and visit before heading home after school.

Judy's grandfather was a retired carpenter, and her grandmother's lap was always available for warmth and comfort. When her parents were too busy, Grandma and Grandpa had all the time in the world to listen.

Because her grandparents blessed her with a sense of belonging, Judy has a strong marriage today and is passing the blessing on to her own children.

*Home is only sweet if we all feel we belong.*

*Is not Ephraim my dear son, the child in whom
I delight?*
—JER. 31:20 NIV

Do you remember how much you delighted in your
son or daughter during those first days of parenthood?
Relatives close at hand came down to ooh and aah at
the baby in the hospital nursery; a flurry of long distance phone calls announced the good news from
coast to coast.

Too soon you realized that even though babies are
fun, they are also a lot of work. After you survived the
terrible twos, fours, and sixes, there may have been
days when you feel like resigning. After surviving
teething and potty training, your children may want
to resign from the human race, too!

How can we make our children feel special?

One dad filled up his little boy's bedroom with balloons. Even though it took him hours to blow up three
hundred balloons, this loving dad thought it was worth
it to see his three-year-old's face light up with wonder
when he awoke that morning.

A mom baked a gigantic chocolate chip cookie (a
foot in diameter) for her daughter's birthday treat, to
share with her classmates. A look at that first grader's
big eyes told everyone how special she felt.

*Lord, how can I delight in my children today?*

*I am the light of the world. He who follows Me
shall not walk in darkness, but have the light
of life.*
                                                    —JOHN 8:12

The Havens children know how highly their mother
values them. They see it every morning as she lights
a prayer candle for each of them. Janet still phones
home from college and says, "Mom, don't let my
prayer candle go out today. I have a tough exam."

The candle is a tangible reminder that Christ is very
active in each child's life. Mom keeps the candles lit as
she prays during the day.

Each candle is a unique representation of the Havens children. Blue-eyed Kathy has a candle decorated
with blue flowers. Skip's is robust in thick-leaded glass.
Multi-colored, cracked glass surrounds James's candle.

Whatever the Havens children are doing, wherever
they are, they know they are being held high in their
mother's heart through prayer.

*Today I will light up the lives of those I love with prayer.*

*He counts the number of the stars; He calls them*
*all by name.*
                                                    —PS. 147:4

Elizabeth had a problem. "I look at something," she explained to her mother, "and my eyes stay there. The kids at school tease me. They call it my staring problem."

Elizabeth's mother smiled. She had noticed that about her daughter too. She liked to gaze out windows. She was a daydreamer. Awestruck. Contemplative. Even as an infant, Elizabeth could sit in front of windows and just quietly look out.

"You know what," Elizabeth's mother said. "There's nothing wrong with you. You are a stargazer. You see things other people don't, and that makes you special. From now on I'm going to call you my Stargazer."

Elizabeth liked that name.

There are unique qualities in our children that are not always easily understood or appreciated. Nurturing parents need to be on the look out for those and treasure them and teach their children to treasure them too.

*Heavenly Father, help me to seek out and cherish the hidden treasures in my children.*

*Thanks be to God for His indescribable gift!*
—2 COR. 9:15

As Debbie drove her daughter to school, she and Zoey talked about Zoey's birthday. Zoey couldn't wait to find out what presents she would get.

"You know," said her mom thoughtfully, "you're a gift to me. Every day this week I'm going to think of one thing I appreciate about you."

There were many things Zoey's mom loved about her daughter, but she didn't often take time to say them. Zoey was the youngest in the family and often felt overlooked. This would be a good opportunity to build her up with praise.

"You know what I love about you?" Debbie said the first day. "I love your infectious smile."

Zoey looked down sheepishly, wondering what that meant.

"That means you pass around joy. When I look at your smile, I feel so happy, I want to smile too."

On other days, Debbie complimented Zoey on her enthusiasm in sports, her careful schoolwork. Zoey was too cool to let her mom know she appreciated the compliments, but Debbie could tell she enjoyed them. As crusty old Mark Twain said, "I can live for two months on one good compliment."

*What gifts our children are, Father. Give me words to speak to them my love.*

*This is My beloved Son. Hear Him!*
—MARK 9:7

One of the ways we can express high value to our loved ones is to give them our undivided attention when we listen to them.

When the phone rang, Steven grabbed it and stuffed it under a pillow. "Dad," he said adamantly, "if you are talking to a member of the community, you are talking to one person. You are talking to me now!" Steven wanted his father's focused attention. He had wanted that all his life. He knew his dad had an important job as mayor of a large suburban city, but wasn't he important too?

"This is My beloved," God pleads. "Listen."

Steven's father, like many parents, might have listened half-heartedly, nodding while talking on the phone, mumbling "uh huh" while reading a magazine or transfixed by TV, but that is clearly not what this desperate son had in mind. Steven ached to be affirmed by his father's attention, to know that he was important and valued. A listening ear communicates acceptance and blessing to those we love.

*Love makes time to listen.*

> *And this I pray, that your love may abound still*
> *more and more in knowledge and all discernment.*
> —PHIL. 1:9

Sometimes we have to listen to what our children don't say even more than what they do say.

Abby was tiptoeing into her little sister's room to get something while Kelsey was napping. "Don't go in there!" Abby's grandmother reprimanded her. "Kelsey has to sleep."

Abby ran into a corner and, crying, buried her head in her knees. Her grandmother apologized for raising her voice, but Abby would not accept her apology.

Abby's mother, Gail, watched all this, sensing that there was something deeper bothering her four-year-old. Gail asked Abby what really was upsetting her.

"I hate Grandma!" Abby cried.

Gail's first reaction was to dismiss her daughter's statement, but instead she asked, "Why do you feel that way?"

Gail discovered that Abby was jealous of all the time Gail and her mother were spending visiting. Abby felt left out. Gail apologized and promised to spend more time with Abby. Understanding her own feelings better, Abby apologized to her grandma.

*Lord, help me to be a discerning listener.*

*The light of the eyes rejoices the heart.*
—PROV. 15:30

Did you know that words comprise only about 7 percent of communication? The rest is body language, tone of voice, and eye contact. A huge amount of talking is done with your eyes.

Have you ever seen a baby sitting in a high chair eagerly waiting for his dad to come home from work? Dad walks through the door and two eyes light up. The little boy bounces up and down in his high chair and his arms shoot out. He's ready for a hug. Does Dad feel like an important person? You bet he does.

Or think of a mom strolling through the grocery store, with a toddler sitting in her cart. The little one's eyes are glued on the most important woman in her life. "Excuse me," says a stranger, "I can't help but notice how much your daughter adores you."

Remember those early days of marriage when Mom and Dad's eyes lit up with the thrill of just looking at each other across a candlelit dinner?

What do your eyes tell your loved ones, now, about your attention barometer?

*Lord, keep my eyes fixed on the most important people in my life.*

*The ears of all the people were attentive.*
—NEH. 8:3

Attentive listening requires a conscious effort to try and understand what other family members are saying. We've developed a method in the Smalley and Trent households that helps us affirm each other and steer clear of conflicts. There are three simple steps:

1. *Try to "see through" to the issue behind the issue.* Honor the other person by letting him clarify what he is saying before responding.

2. *Restate, in your own words, what the other person has said.* By reiterating what you just heard the speaker say, you are letting him know if you received his message. Ask questions and reword the statement until the speaker acknowledges, "Yes, that's it."

3. *Lovingly limit your own words.* In an important discussion, it's good to remember not to use too many words. Meandering can tune a listener out, especially children with short attention spans!

Improving listening skills can go a long way in strengthening family communication.

*Make me an attentive listener, Lord.*

*Finally, brethren, whatever things are true,*
*whatever things are noble, whatever things are*
*just, whatever things are pure, whatever things*
*are lovely, whatever things are of good report,*
*if there is any virtue and if there is anything*
*praiseworthy—meditate on these things.*

—PHIL. 4:8

Children flourish under praise. To accentuate the positive, try a drumroll at dinnertime. Instead of reporting the worst behavior of the day, and thus reinforcing it, beat your fingertips on the table and proclaim an outstanding achievement for each child:

"Jody made her own bed without being told to."

"Glenn resolved a fight between friends. He's becoming a peacemaker!"

"Chris helped watch the neighbor's kids while their mom was busy."

We need to celebrate each other's achievements—however modest. Too often, our day is focused on the negative, correcting children, scolding, getting down on them. They begin to wonder if they can do anything right!

Praising our children is a way of saluting their efforts, holding them in high esteem, valuing who they are and what they are becoming.

*Lord, help me to catch my children doing something right today and praise them for it!*

> *The lips of the righteous nourish many.*
> —PROV. 10:21 NIV

Words of praise can nourish our children's self-worth. The more specific the praise, the more effective it will be.

A kindergartner comes home with a picture from school. Mom may be affirming. "That's a great picture!" But a little more attention would show how highly Mom values the picture and the little person who made it. Taking Jamie up into her lap, she could wrap loving arms around her son and study his creation. "I really like the way you used yellow and blue in your picture. I notice you're coloring in the lines better, too."

Walking away from a softball game, a mother of an eleven-year-old praises her daughter, "You played a super game, honey."

But the compliment doesn't mean much because the daughter knows her mom was talking to the other parents and really hadn't watched the game at all.

Specific praise—"you really had to work to catch that fly ball in the third inning"—would show genuine attentiveness and encouragement.

---

*Specific praise hits the target of the heart with life-giving accuracy.*

*Let her . . . works praise her in the gates.*
—PROV. 31:31

Good job!" You can say it with words and you can say it other ways. Andrea knew she had done a good job every time she walked in the front door of her house. On the wall in front of her were construction paper cut-outs, pictures she had colored, a mask she had made. Her "art gallery" was in the most prominent part of the house, where everyone could applaud it.

Rachel, on the other hand, was a little girl who never saw her artwork up on a wall. Thirty years later she remembers, "My mom never put one of my pictures up because she wanted her house to be perfect and my pictures did not match her decor. If I brought home a clay bowl I had made, she stuck it in a box and put it out of sight."

It is said that actions speak louder than words. These wordless actions do speak a message loud and clear. A message of depreciation, "You're not very important around here." Or a message of praise, "You're special and we treasure who you are."

*Help me to applaud my children by giving them a prominent place in my life, Lord.*

> *Therefore encourage one another and build each*
> *other up.*                              —1 THESS. 5:11 NIV

It is easier to tear down, than to build up. Just listen to your children at the dinner table, taking jabs at each other. "That was a stupid thing to say." "Don't you know anything?" Or listen to them talk about classmates, "You should see the clothes she wears, and the way he walks!"

As children get older, peers applaud them for the cleverness of their put-downs. "My that's a nice ring you have on," says a seventh-grade girl, "did you get it from a gum ball machine?" If someone calls you a dog and says, "Whoof-whoof," the retaliatory phrase is, "Look who's barking!" These satirical barbs, called "burns," aim to devalue. Even though tossed around in jest, they hurt.

One way to counter this tendency is to require your children to redress a put-down with a "put up." For example, if one sibling insults another, ask the offender to apologize and to compliment the offended. Watch the struggle to come up with something positive. "I like the way you fixed your hair today," and see how a frown can turn to a smile.

*Lord, help me to build people up today and encourage my children to affirm others.*

*Nevertheless let each one of you in particular so love his own wife as himself, and let the wife see that she respects her husband.* —EPH. 5:33

It has been said that the best thing we can do for our children is to love our spouse. There are opportunities every day for husbands and wives to elevate each other in front of their children.

An angry daughter is disgruntled with her father. "He's mean! He's unfair!"

This is when a mom can be supportive. She can explain Dad's point of view: why he meted out discipline as he did, how his actions, which may appear negative to a self-centered child, are motivated by love.

The next time, it might be Dad's turn to uphold Mom. A disrespectful son snaps back at his mother. Dad steps in. "Son, you should respect your mother. Please use another tone of voice when speaking to her."

Our parental authority, which is certain to be attacked, is much stronger when both parents work together to hold the line.

And what better way for our children to learn to bless those they love than to see parents affirming each other and holding one another in high regard?

*Lord, thank You for giving me a husband who esteems me in front of my children; help me to show him the same respect.*

> *Honor your father and your mother.*
> —DEUT. 5:16

The surest way to devalue a parent is for one spouse to dishonor the other in front of their children.

Rob and Diane were at a Christian family camp. Rob had taken the children on a hike through the woods so Diane could rest. When they came back to the cabin, Courtney, five, was crying because she had stepped in a mud puddle and gotten her new sandals dirty. Diane glared at Rob. "You should have put her tennis shoes on."

"You didn't tell me to," Rob fired back.

Their discussion became more heated. They could have simply washed the sandals, but instead, both parents became coldly critical of each other.

The camp speaker had been focusing on compassion. Diane was suddenly aware of how little compassion she felt for her husband. It was a dark, ugly thing to admit, but she harbored resentment toward Rob for past mistakes and didn't want God to bless him through her.

Convicted of her judgmental and critical attitude, she apologized to Rob.

---

*Do I let negative feelings toward my husband dishonor him in front of my children?*

*In everything give thanks.*
—1 THESS. 5:18

One way we can value our loved ones is to express our appreciation for how they bless us. "My marriage is a lot like a raft trip," a thankful husband told his wife. "There are times when I take us down an uncharted section of the river, and we overturn and everything gets soaked. But I never hear you complain. I know I tend to go off on new ideas without looking at a map, but you never hold it against me. I know I'm blessed to have you." Word pictures are a poignant way to communicate high value to a spouse we esteem.

Another wife used her husband's birthday to express appreciation. She listed his special qualities with a brief explanation beside each attribute. Beside "Depth," she wrote: "A friend once said you reminded her of the saying, 'still waters run deep.' In conversation she noticed that everyone talked while you were silent. Then you contributed something that exactly hit home. I notice that too. I admire your restraint and continue to learn from it."

We need to value each other for who we are, not just for what we do.

*Today I will give thanks for my loved ones and let them know how much they mean to me.*

> *A good man out of the good treasure of his heart*
> *brings forth good. . . . For out of the abundance of*
> *the heart his mouth speaks.*  —LUKE 6:45

The Bible says that our words and actions spring from the heart, where our attitudes are formed. If we fill the storehouse of our minds with good thoughts, blessing is bound to spill out. In the same way, focusing on negative thoughts produces words and actions that devalue those we love.

It is easy to dwell on hurtful memories and let hard feelings affect our present attitudes. Recalling good memories can be equally powerful in making present attitudes more positive.

Evonne had been overly critical of her husband lately. To curb that destructive attitude, Evonne asked Jesus to bring to mind a good memory of Steve. Suddenly she remembered a tender moment when Steve had taken her and the children to the train station. She was so full of love for him. It was to be a long train ride and Steve had bought the children bags of special treats. He was such a good provider and she tended to take that for granted. That warm memory acted as a springboard to fill Evonne's mind with good thoughts. As she began to bless Steve in her heart, her actions also became more honoring.

*Lord, teach me to store away good memories of happy days to bless the rainy days that will come.*

*As the Father loved Me, I also have loved you; abide
in My love.*                                    —JOHN 15:9

As mothers and wives, it is easy to be so intent on
blessing our children and husbands that we forget to
take time to bless ourselves.

This really came home to Carey when her five-year-
old showed her a picture of a house in heaven. It
showed a beautiful house with flowers on the window
sill and three people with smiling faces riding in a jew-
eled horse-drawn coach, eagerly coming home.

"That's great, honey. There's Daddy and you and
your brother, but where is Mommy?"

Her little girl grinned. "Cleaning the house!"

Carey laughed. That was not *her* idea of heaven. But
she had to admit that was how her daughter often saw
her: cleaning, cooking, meeting the family's needs.

She used to enjoy taking long leisurely baths; now
she took quick showers. When she was pregnant, she
napped if she was tired "for the baby's sake." She could
never do that now without feeling guilty.

But Jesus invited her to "abide," to rest and relax in
His love. That afternoon she enjoyed a long, soaking
bubble bath. At this time Carey blessed herself by meditating and praying as she relaxed.

*Today I will take time to bless myself.*

*Since you were precious in My sight, you have been
honored, and I have loved you.*              —ISA. 43:4

A friend told Judith that when she was searching for
a card to send someone, she often bought a card for
herself and pasted it in her devotional journal. Her
friend showed her the picture of a little girl smelling a
beautiful spring flower. The caption read, "I appreciate
you." "I think God meant that message for me," she
said, "so I bought that card and kept it."

"Oh, I could never do that!" Judith shrieked. "Spend
a dollar and a half on myself!"

Judith, who had been taught to put the needs of
others over her own, balked at the thought of such ex-
travagance. It seemed wasteful to spend a few dollars
on herself.

Judith would find it difficult to drink in the words
of high value God is speaking to us today. "You are
precious . . . you are honored . . . I love you." Those
words were meant for her and they are meant for you.
God loves you, apart from the roles you play: mother,
wife, teacher, caregiver, community or church leader.
In God's eyes, you are a precious, many splendored
creation, deserving of honor and praise—just because
you're you.

*Take joy in who you are!*

*I will praise You, for I am fearfully and
wonderfully made.*                      **—PS. 139:14**

When someone admires your child, how does it make
you feel? A stranger stops you in the store and says,
"What gorgeous eyes your daughter has." Or an admiring parent on the sidelines comments, "Boy, can your
kid run." How does it make you feel? Proud? Honored?
When we take joy in who *we* are that's how God, our
proud papa, feels.

Margaret was surprised one day, overhearing her
seven-year-old daughter brushing her hair in the bathroom. "I look so stupid!" her daughter snarled at herself. "My hair is so dumb! I hate myself!"

Margaret, who worked hard to build up her daughter, couldn't believe how viciously she was tearing herself down.

But then she thought about her own self-talk. Noticing her reflection in a store window, she would sigh,
"You look terrible." Or upon making a mistake, she
would be merciless, "You are so stupid!"

If we are lovely enough for God to embrace and
cherish, shouldn't we hold ourselves in high regard?

*Oh, heavenly Father, teach me to embrace myself with love as
You do.*

*But if a woman has long hair, it is a glory to her.*
—1 COR. 11:15

I just love being with women," said Suzanne, who was looking forward to attending a women's retreat. Suzanne was the mother of two boys. With three men in the family, she was outnumbered. "I often feel so alone."

Her friend listened in amazement. "It's funny you should say that," said Marcia. "My mother-in-law has three sons and she used to tell me how wonderful it was to finally have a daughter in the family. I had long hair and she used to enjoy brushing it. Actually it kind of embarrassed me."

Suzanne smiled. "You must have given her great joy."

Marcia remembered back twenty years to the days her mother-in-law would stroke her hair so lovingly. Marcia hadn't thought of her hair as beautiful. She wore it long to cover up her many fears. She had been insecure about people looking at her. She had been uncertain about her femininity. It took someone else to appreciate the glory of who she was. The next time she saw her mother-in-law, she would give her a big hug of thanks.

————————

*You crown me with glory, Lord. Today I will walk like a queen.*

# A PENNY FOR YOUR THOUGHTS – *April 27*

> *He [Jesus] saw also a certain poor widow putting in*
> *two mites [to the treasury]. So He said, ". . . this*
> *poor widow has put in more than all."*
> —LUKE 21:2-3

Jesus valued small things. He valued the widow's contribution because it represented great love and sacrifice. He said that even a little faith could move a mountain and He compared the kingdom of heaven to a mustard seed.

If Jesus walked among us today, He probably would not pass a penny on the sidewalk because of its little value.

Neither did Janet. In fact, she decided to take some pennies and paste a tiny red felt heart on each one. Then she put the pennies in various jeans and skirt pockets. She would forget about them until at some moment during the day she would slip her hand into her pocket and feel one there.

She would smile to herself. Each penny was a reminder of how much God loved her. On bad days, especially when she felt very small and worthless, her pennies would lift her spirits.

---

*A penny for Your thoughts, Lord. They make me feel like a million dollars!*

*I have come that they may have life, and that they may have it more abundantly. I am the good shepherd.*
                                    —JOHN 10:10–11

Donna was in despair. It was her birthday and no one seemed to notice. Her husband was leaving on a business trip and was oblivious to Donna's special day.

At seven in the morning, the phone rang. "Happy birthday to you!" sang Donna's parents.

Knowing it was a hard day, her mom called back later. Donna still felt low. "You know," said her mom, "people don't make celebrations special. The Shepherd does. It took me sixty-three years to find that out."

She told Donna that last year she didn't have anyone close to help celebrate her birthday. "You have to take what is in your hand and let the Lord bless it." Instead of feeling sorry for herself, she took a cake and celebration to a friend's house.

Donna's mom then shared a Bible verse about the abundant life Jesus promises. Donna's outlook changed. Instead of dwelling on what she didn't have, Donna began to focus on what she did have. She was richly blessed with health, loved ones, material comforts . . .

---

*Count your many blessings, see what God has done.*

*Oh come, let us worship and bow down; let us
kneel before the LORD our Maker.*   —PS. 95:6

To *bless* literally means to "bow the knee," showing
reverence and honor to an important person. Certainly
no person is more important in our lives than the One
who made us.

Kathy felt stressed out. When her life was simpler,
B.C. (Before Children), she had enjoyed worshiping
God during quiet times. But, little by little, her many
demands edged that precious time out. As she lost that
time to rest in God's presence, she felt more and more
overburdened.

While she was praying one day, God showed Kathy
a picture of a wheel. She was the hub of the wheel and
the wheel itself seemed to represent the circle of relationships that spun around her. Having placed herself
at the center of the wheel, responsible for everyone
else's needs, her own needs were not being met. She
realized that God needed to be at the center.

One of the ways Kathy put God back in the center
of her life was to reestablish a consistent quiet time. It
didn't have to be long, perhaps only ten minutes, but
it served to provide the balance in her life that was
missing.

*Is God at the center of your life, or the periphery?*

*Great is the LORD, and greatly to be praised.*
—PS.145:3

Worship is uplifting. One day Jean noticed a poster hanging on the wall beside the dining room table where she had devotions. Entitled *Morning Flight*, the poster portrayed a dozen hot-air balloons floating serenely above spacious countryside, green and still.

That picture seemed to capture exactly what worship did for her: she would come burdened, preoccupied with looming problems. As she contemplated the greatness of God, she would release her problems and allow the Holy Spirit's flame to fill her with the warm energy of His love. Up, up and away she'd go.

What a different perspective she had from God's point of view! Cares and worries that seemed insurmountable suddenly shrunk. She couldn't handle them, but He could. His love was so great, so vast—limitless. Jean felt free as she sensed God's Spirit, so fresh, so full of power.

*Today I will let God's love lift me above life's circumstances.*

*Bless the Lord, O my soul; and all that is within
me, bless His holy name!*
                                                    —PS. 103:1

One of the ways we can bless God is to appreciate
who He is. Various names in the Bible reveal different
aspects of His character. As we meditate on these
names, praising God for who He is, we, too, are
blessed as we realize His resources are ours.

One of the Hebrew names for God is *Jehovah-Jireh*,
meaning "God our provider." Praise God for being
your provider. He not only supplies our material needs,
but He redeems us from whatever mistakes we make.

*Jehovah-Shammah* means "God is present." God
promises always to be with us to comfort, to
strengthen, to guide. Praise God for walking close beside you like a friend. Enjoy His companionship the
whole day through.

*Jehovah-Shalom*, "God is our peace," speaks of the
deep tranquility God can bring. As you say this name,
say it slowly and let God's Spirit infuse you with a
sense of wholeness and well-being.

*Jehovah-Rophi* means "the Lord who heals." God
hurts when we hurt and He longs to see us healthy and
happy. He is able to heal broken bodies and broken
hearts.

———————

*I exalt You, Lord, and lift Your name in praise.*

*Bless the LORD, O my soul, and forget not all His benefits.*
—PS. 103:2

Mary was exhausted. It was the morning after Erica's birthday party. Pizza, pop, games, and ten nine-year-olds whispering and giggling in sleeping bags all night. One was hungry at midnight. Another was afraid of the dark. Down to and up from the basement, Mary had marched all night.

"Aren't you forgetting something?" Mary eyed Erica.

Erica looked up from her new toys, unresponsive.

"Your birthday party was a lot of work," said Mary.

A light bulb went on in Erica's head. She smiled. "Oh, thanks, Mom."

It seems like we have to remind our children endlessly to say thank you, but how appreciative are we? We plead passionately for God to answer prayer; when He does, we are already preoccupied with another concern. We take for granted benefits which come our way, forgetting they are gifts.

God's gifts are so great—forgiveness, mercy, salvation—we should stand in awe, in gratitude. Another way to bless God is to say thanks. After Jesus healed ten lepers, only one returned to express his appreciation. "Where are the other nine?" Jesus asked (Luke 17:17).

———

*Oh, Lord, forgive me for forgetting to say thank You. You have blessed me so greatly.*

*Surely, the smell of my son is like the smell of a
field which the LORD has blessed. . . . Let peoples
serve you, and nations bow down to you.*
—GEN. 27:27, 29

A fourth element of giving the blessing is to picture
a special future for those we bless. This is not only to
appreciate how special our loved ones are, but also to
inspire them to be all they can be.

Isaac's blessing to Jacob suggests how highly he re-
garded his son. Isaac uses a word picture to describe
how unique and special Jacob is, then he enhances this
by saying his son is so special whole nations will one
day honor him.

We all need to know we are somebody, V.I.P.'s. Our
family members especially need to know how highly
we value them. We need to affirm the gifts in those we
love and encourage them to realize their full potential.
We can't leave that important job to someone else.

The world our children live in can be uncaring and
humiliating at times. Our spouses' work can be hard
and demanding. In light of this, it is crucial that our
homes be nurturing places where we bring out the best
in each other, launching pads from which we can take
off for the stars.

*Lord, make me a possibility thinker today.*

> *For I know the thoughts that I think toward you,*
> *says the* LORD, *thoughts of peace and not of evil,*
> *to give you a future and a hope.* —JER. 29:11

Picturing a special future for a child, a spouse, or friend can help bring out the best in them. "Treat a person as he appears to be," said Goethe, "and you make him worse. But treat a person as if he already were what he potentially could be and you make him what he should be."

Jesus understood this important truth when he changed Simon's name to Peter, meaning *rock*. The impetuous, shaky disciple certainly didn't feel solid himself, much less capable of forging the foundation of the church! Yet, at Pentecost, he became as bold as Jesus had predicted because someone he loved had seen the best in him.

Carrie's parents gave her the middle name "Alexandra" because it meant *helper of mankind*. They hoped Carrie would grow up wanting to help others, but they never dreamed how quickly she would take her name to heart. As early as three or four, Carrie would complete a chore and announce proudly, "I am Carrie Alexandra, the man-helper."

Loving words that picture a special future for our children have tremendous power to help them reach toward the best in themselves.

---

*Do I see my children as they are, or as they could be?*

*A good name is better than precious ointment.*
—ECCL. 7:1

Letting your child know why you named him what you did can be a great encouragement, especially if there is special significance behind it.

I (Gary) learned this when my son, Greg, was eighteen. As a freshman in college, Greg was given the assignment of researching his family tree. He found old photos and letters from relatives I didn't even know we had kept.

He found a letter buried in a closet that particularly intrigued him. It was a letter I had written to him, explaining why we had given him the name we did. I had discovered that Cardinal Hildebrand, the eleventh-century clergyman who became Pope Gregory VII, was an ancestor of ours. At seminary, I learned that Gregory was a man with a personal, vibrant relationship with Christ. I was impressed with his character traits and wanted to build them into my son.

As I shared these things about the man whose name he carried, I could see that Greg felt honored. Knowing these things helped my son answer the question, "Who am I?" and pointed to high aspirations that inspired what he could be.

*Lord, help me to let my children know how highly I view them.*

> *I will bless you and make your name great; and*
> *you shall be a blessing.*
> —GEN. 12:2

The Coelho girls know they are special and greatly loved. They know this because on the day they were born, their grandfather gave them Hawaiian names that carried a blessing.

Christiana Joy's name is Meleokalani, which means *Song of heaven.* "Christiana always has had music in her heart," says her mom. "As a toddler, she danced to the radio. She played piano at four and has had a passion for music."

Ashely Nicole Kapiolani is named for the godly Hawaiian queen, Kapiolani, who first opened up the door of the islands to missionaries. Her name means *Gateway to heaven.* "Ashely," says her mother, "is strongwilled and fearless and stands strong for Jesus, even now."

Rebecca Jean's Hawaiian name is Alohalani, which means *Love of heaven.* Just like her name, she is tender and loving.

Each of the girls' Hawaiian names ends with the word Lani, which means *heaven.* As their grandfather had hoped, their heavenly names have blessed them with a special future and made them a blessing to others.

———

*Lord, help me to instill in my children a picture of what they can become.*

*Beloved, now we are children of God; and it has not yet been revealed what we shall be, but we know that when He is revealed, we shall be like Him.*
                                                                    —1 JOHN 3:2

To instill Christlike traits into their children, Alice and Tom felt it was important to find a tangible symbol that represented the best in each of them.

When Elizabeth was baptized, she was given a little sheep as a reminder that she had become a child of God. Elizabeth has a picture on her bedroom wall of Jesus carrying a lamb in His arms. She is developing a tender heart like the Good Shepherd's. On every birthday, Elizabeth's parents give her a new lamb figurine with a note celebrating who she is.

In the ninth grade, Randy avidly read the Tolkein trilogy. He was given a large, wax figure of Gandolf, a man of trust and nobility. Such were the character traits his parents hoped to form in him.

James was fond of the Narnia books and the Christlike figure of the lion, Aslan. James's symbol is the lion representing the gentle strength of Christ.

Symbols can provide visions that help shape the lives of our children for good.

*Lord, help me to surround my children with positive images, images that capture Your highest dreams for them.*

> *And I will write on him My new name.*
> —REV. 3:12

Jim Jones had an unremarkable name—until it became a household word associated with poisoned Kool-aid and the mass suicide of nine hundred people in Guyana. Jim, a gentle husband and loving father, resented being linked with the fanatical cult leader, just because of his name. Any time he gave his name, people would immediately crack jokes about him. Jim laughed good-naturedly, but inside he was hurting.

Then one morning in a Sunday school class, Jim met a woman named Sally. When Jim introduced himself, Sally could see that the subject of his name was a painful subject.

"You know," she smiled, "God can give you a new name."

Sally asked if she could pray with Jim. In prayer, she affirmed Jim as a man with a heart for God and saw "rivers of living water flowing out of him. You are a source of life to other people, a source of purity and refreshment, Jim."

Sally's prayer went deep and began a work of inner transformation that gave him a whole new picture of himself.

---

*Lord, is there someone I know who would flourish with a new name? If so, let me affirm the good in them.*

*You who seek the LORD: look to the rock from
which you were hewn.*                    —ISA. 51:1

Word pictures can be a powerful way to picture a special future for someone.

As a mother of two children under the age of three, Jenny was devastated when her husband divorced her. With no marketable skills or job experience, she faced one struggle after another. Today, six years later, Jenny has a good job that pays the bills, yet allows her time to spend with her children. We asked her to identify her greatest source of help during those first hard years.

"The Lord was certainly the greatest source of help to us when Jack first left; but from a human perspective, I would have to point to my father. Every time I wanted to quit school or just give up, he would say to me, 'You'll make it, Jenny. You're my rock of Gibraltar. I know you'll make it.'

"I didn't feel like a rock at the time. My whole world seemed to be caving in. But it helped to know that he pictured me this way. It gave me the hope that maybe I could make it."

We can give this same hope to others when we use word pictures that point out abilities or strengths they might not be aware of.

───────────

*"You can make it!" Lord, does someone need to hear that from me today?*

> *Therefore if anyone is in Christ, he is a new creation; old things have passed away; behold, all things have become new.* —2 COR. 5:17

Adolesence is often the most painful time of growing up. It certainly was for Milly. She still remembers the night she came home from a junior high dance, shattered. No one had asked this tall, gawky teenager to dance. She was mortified.

Milly's father met her at the door when she came home. If he had ignored the hurt in Milly's eyes, she would have escaped up to bed and cried herself to sleep. But he didn't. He listened patiently while Milly told him how miserable she was.

"Life isn't fair," sobbed Milly.

Her dad agreed, then told her about the humiliation and rejection he had suffered while growing up. But he assured Milly that one day boys would be lined up at the door. He reminded her of the story of the ugly duckling whose awkwardness only lasted a short time. Someday, he promised, she would be a swan.

Then Milly's father took her hand and asked her to dance. As she glided across the living room in her father's arms, Milly felt cherished and beautiful—like a new creation.²

*Lord, help our children see the future through eyes of love.*

*The LORD is faithful to all his promises . . .*
—PS. 145:13 NIV

Ted did a good job of picturing a special future for his children, but his words were never matched with actions. Noticing that his daughter loved animals, he promised to buy her a horse. "You might even become a veterinarian some day." He told his son, Bobby, that he was so talented at baseball that he might even be a pro player. He promised to throw grounders with Bobby as soon as he had time.

But as a traveling salesman, Ted never could find time to be with his children. After nine years of being on the road, Ted finally realized he had to make changes to build a secure family life.

He got a new job which allowed him to stay home— even though it meant a cut in pay. The first thing he did was buy his daughter a horse, but she was no longer interested in horses, and Bobby had lost his interest in baseball.

Ted regretted his many years of empty promises, but he truly loved his wife and children. God helped Ted become a faithful father and husband, but it took time. It took Ted two years of consistently keeping promises to assure his family that he really did want the best for their future.

———————

*Words of a special future need to be backed up by honoring commitments today.*

## *May 12* – TAKING THE LONG VIEW

*Let your eyes look straight ahead.*
—PROV. 4:25

Picturing a special future for our children means taking the long view, keeping our eyes fixed on a goal—even if it seems unattainable.

When Marcia told her parents she wanted to be a teacher one day, they could have dismissed her dream as nonsense. Labeled a "slow learner," Marcia was always at the bottom of her class. They could have said, "Now, Marcia, let's be realistic."

But instead of laughing, Marcia's parents dug in their heels and got to work helping Marcia realize her dream. In spite of her poor academic record, Marcia could explain things to younger children in ways they could understand. Her parents affirmed these gifts and encouraged her.

Marcia struggled through school. She was tutored in grade school and attended special reading classes in high school. It took her six-and-a-half years to complete a four-year college program, but she made it. While most of her classmates were looking for jobs, Marcia already had one. She had done such an outstanding job student teaching that the principal of the school where she taught offered her a full-time position.

*How can I use words of blessing to help my children realize their full potential?*

*But one thing I do, forgetting those things which
are behind and reaching forward to those things
which are ahead, I press toward the goal. . . .*
                                        —PHIL. 3:13–14

One of the best ways to picture a special future for
our children is to focus on their successes instead of
their failures. The way to do it is, as Paul says, forget
what is behind and reach toward what is ahead.

When Molly moved to a new school in the third
grade, she was completely demoralized. Her new
school was much more demanding academically and
she quickly fell behind. Her parents knew that leaving
behind old friends and everything that was familiar
was hard enough for Molly. In the light of those struggles, feeling like a failure in the classroom was a crush-
ing blow to her self-esteem.

To encourage Molly, her parents put her best school
papers up on the refrigerator where she could see
them every day. The rest were thrown away. What a
difference! As Molly looked at those papers, she began
to see herself as a success rather than a failure. Gradually, her schoolwork improved. "Outstanding" and
"wow" began to appear on the papers on the frig.

*I will focus on my children's successes today.*

> *Blessed is she who believed, for there will be a fulfillment of those things which were told her from the Lord.*
>
> —LUKE 1:45

It is helpful while envisioning a special future for our children to be encouraged in the here and now.

"Mom," said Brenna, "what does it feel like to have your dream come true?"

"What do you mean, Brenna?" Betsy looked puzzled. In the midst of doing the dishes, that seemed like a faraway question.

Brenna read a line out of a book Betsy had written twelve years before. "I hoped my baby would mature into a happy, caring individual, one who would embrace life openly and love others." Brenna looked up, smiling. "That happened, right?"

Betsy was caught short. She had written those words while pregnant with Brenna. She had hoped that one day her daughter would read those lines about herself. Her dream *had* come true. Brenna was soft and compassionate and as loving as she had hoped she would be.

"Mom," said Brenna. "Why are you crying?"[3]

---

*While dreaming of what they'll become, I'll also celebrate who my children are now.*

*And Jesus increased in wisdom and stature, and in favor with God and men.*                    —LUKE 2:52

We can celebrate our children's successes daily, but there are special opportunities—milestones like turning a certain age, graduating from school, winning a certain award—that provide an ideal time to affirm our children's progress.

One father found a unique way to mark a milestone in his daughters' lives. As Old Testament parents marked their children's coming of age with a special ceremony of blessing, this father took each daughter out on a special date on her sixteenth birthday.

On this special date, Dad walked up the sidewalk with a corsage, took his date to a special restaurant, and gave her a prayer list for the family he hoped she would have in years to come.

"After my sixteen-candle dinner with my father, I felt for the first time like I was really growing up," one daughter recalls. "We talked about some of the responsibilities, like dating and driving, I had ahead of me, and it really helped me realize it was time to grow up."

Celebrating moments of maturity allows our children to move on with confidence.

---

*Lord, help me to give my children a sense of accomplishment to build on throughout their lives.*

*Let your heart retain my words; keep my
commands, and live.*
—PROV. 4:4

John was caught in the crossfire of a bloody civil war
in a country far removed from the Illinois farmland
where he grew up. Risking his life to interview soldiers
on both sides of the conflict, he was determined to get
the truth out in a news story that would capture the
world's attention and bring help to this beleaguered
nation where thousands of refugees were trapped and
dying.

Why had he chosen so dangerous a calling when he
could have eased into a comfortable job after college?
"Because I want to leave the world a better place than
I found it," said John, recalling the words of his father
and grandfather.

Those words had become a family motto handed
down through three generations. Grandpa Jenkins, a
teacher on a modest salary, used to take his three sons
camping. When they broke camp, he would always tell
the boys to pick up the trash, even though it wasn't all
theirs. "You need to leave the campground better than
you found it."

Those words, that high ethic, lodged in the heart of
John's father and they stuck with John. Over the years,
they shaped his life and his destiny.

*What family mottos do you have that can inspire the best in your
children?*

*Train up a child in the way he should go, and*
*when he is old he will not depart from it.*
—PROV. 22:6

When parents are raising their young children, the future seems very far off. Parents of adult children, however, will tell you that looking back from their perspective, the time went very quickly.

That is why Solomon, the wisest man on earth, suggested that planning for the future begins today. Training up a child involves setting goals for our child's "going" from the earliest years.

Every day you have a child in your home there are opportunities to prepare him for the future. Ask yourself questions like, "What can I teach my child about finances today that will help him be capable of handling his own finances later?" Opening a checking account or giving him a budget to plan his expenses are helpful ways to teach money management.

Opportunities come each day to teach responsibility. If a child forgets to lock his bike and it's stolen, have him save the money to replace it instead of buying him a new one.

Confirming your child's right choices and helping him analyze and learn from mistakes in the present will pay dividends in the future.

*Lord, give me wisdom to capture each teachable moment.*

*Make plans by seeking advice.*
—PROV. 20:18 NIV

How can we help our children reach their own goals? My (Gary's) son Michael decided he wanted to play football. Long before the season started, we sat down together for a few hours and drew out a conditioning and skill-building plan. I asked him questions like, "How much time are you willing to put into developing skills you need to strengthen? An hour a week? Five hours a month? Do you want me to ask you once a week how you're doing? Once a month?"

These things gave him a goal he could shoot for and gave him confidence in knowing that he was organized in his efforts, not just shooting in the dark. After I helped Mike establish his goals, we wrote up what we had agreed on in a contract that we both signed.

Norma and I have done similar things with all our children: with Kari, concerning the kind of person she wants to date; with Greg on his choice of vocation; and with all of them concerning spiritual goals.

Helping a child establish a plan to reach his goals instills in him a sense of success he will carry into adulthood.

_____

*What can I do today to help my children make their dreams come true?*

*Where there is no vision, the people perish.*
—PROV. 29:18 KJV

When Lynn pictured a special future for her daughters, she hoped for marriage for them. She had prayed since the girls were born that they would someday find loving husbands, committed to the same ideals as they.

"Mom," her twelve-year-old said one day, "I think everybody is going to be divorced by the time I grow up." Stacy often came home from school and told her mom about friends whose parents were splitting up or living with different partners. What a contrast to her own youth when she had not known even one family ripped apart by divorce until going to college. Once the exception, now divorce was nearing the norm.

Was God's plan for marriage as a lifetime commitment just an old-fashioned idea taught in Sunday school? Lynn realized that if she were to show her daughters how fulfilling Christian marriage could be, she needed to do more than pray and wait for their future to unfold. She needed to make her marriage the best it could be because the picture of marriage they viewed now would provide their vision for stepping into that same future some day.

---

*There is much that can be done today to influence what happens tomorrow.*

> *Better is a dry morsel with quietness, than a house*
> *full of feasting with strife.*
> —PROV. 17:1

Dana had always admired the house on the hill with its large picture windows overlooking a lovely lake. *How restful it must be to live up there,* she thought. *Those people must be on top of the world!*

She would never have guessed that one day she would be driving up to that very house to answer a distress call. One Sunday after Dana had taught a class at church on healing unhealthy relationships, a woman approached her. She told Dana about her troubled marriage, then asked if Dana would consider coming to her house to counsel and pray with her.

When Dana walked into the expensive, contemporary home, she found that it was anything but restful. Anger and bitterness had filled the house with violence, ripping apart a marriage. Mom and Dad screamed at each other and the children took refuge in their bedrooms, behind closed doors.

Is your home filled with quietness or strife? Our children need more from parents than a roof over their heads. They need a place of quietness and peace to rest secure and feel safe to dream.

*Lord, help me to provide my family a safe house where they can fashion special futures.*

*The rain descended, the floods came, and the winds blew and beat on that house; and it did not fall, for it was founded on the rock.*

—MATT. 7:25

Children need to know that their homes are built on a firm foundation, not shifting sand.

In our book *The Language of Love,* we tell the story of a husband and wife. We could do nothing to convince them to stop their heated arguments until their children were invited into the discussion.

"What bothers you the most about your parents' arguing?" we asked their six-year-old daughter.

"Every time Daddy gets mad at Mommy or us, he takes off his wedding ring and throws it away."

The little girl's father quickly explained that he did that just to vent his anger. He wasn't literally throwing his wedding ring away.

But to her it was real enough. Every time she saw her daddy's ring go flying across the room, she saw her future sail away with it. Her father's gesture created so much insecurity that she had already been diagnosed as having childhood ulcers.

Mom and Dad finally realized how deeply they were damaging their children. This little girl's insight provided the impetus her parents needed to work toward restoring their marriage.

*Heavenly Father, help my words and actions to build security into my children's lives.*

> *The LORD is my rock . . . ; my strength, in whom I will trust.*
> —PS. 18:2

No parent is perfect. Even with the best intentions, there are times we all fail our children. When our lives are strong and certain, we may be able to provide the security our children need, but often parents are struggling with their own insecurities. At those times, we need the help of a loving heavenly Father whose love is changeless, solid, firm as a rock.

Wise parents know that any strength they have to bestow the blessing on their children comes from an all-powerful God. Even the very breath of life they have to speak words of blessing comes from Him.

The most special future parents can picture for their children is one based on God's love, the one thing that will never fail them.

Is the future of your children founded on the Rock? Do they have a special Friend who will always be there to walk close to encourage, comfort and strengthen them throughout their lives?

---

*What can I do today to draw them closer to the Father?*

*His faithfulness continues through all generations.*
—PS. 100:5 NIV

Our children need to know that God confirms our blessing and will help us carry it out—even if we're not there.

At forty-one, Ray died suddenly of a massive heart attack. Karen and Nicole no longer had their father's arms to comfort them or his affirming words to bless them. However, they still felt comforted and affirmed because their father had told them that Jesus would continue to do that.

In *The Blessing,* we recount the words of Ray's widow, Lisa. "Before Ray died, he used to gather us all together right before dinner. We would all get in a little circle, holding each other's hands. Then Papa would pray and thank the Lord for our day and for the food. He would end each prayer by squeezing my hand and saying, 'Lord Jesus, thank You that You are Karen's, and Nicole's, and Lisa's, and my Shepherd. Thank You that You will never leave us or forsake us. Amen.' It's been rough this past year without Ray, but it has helped so much to be able to remind the children that Jesus is still their Shepherd as well as their father's."

*Oh, Father, thank You that I can draw on Your faithfulness to bless my children even beyond my human efforts.*

> *Therefore we also, since we are surrounded by so
> great a cloud of witnesses, . . . let us run with
> endurance the race that is set before us.*
> —HEB. 12:1

In the race of life, just as in any marathon, there are casualties and injuries, mishaps that prevent even the best runners from continuing the race. A Christian can take heart that he runs in Christ's strength and never alone.

When a family member is lost, sometimes the whole foundation of the family threatens to crumble. This was true in the Meyers' case. When her dearly loved father died, Mrs. Meyers, the family provider, had a nervous breakdown. Her husband, Greg, trying to finish up a college degree, to establish a new mid-life career, was so discouraged and behind in his courses that he was ready to throw in the towel. He felt he just couldn't go on with college.

Then a check came. An old family friend, who knew how much Mrs. Meyers' father had valued his son-in-law's education, asked that the money be used to help Greg complete his degree. "The best memorial for Gordon," wrote the friend, "is for Greg to get his degree."

That gift of hope gave Greg the courage to keep on running.

_____

*Lord, thanks for the encouragers in my life who have spurred me on
when I felt like giving up.*

*Unless the LORD builds the house, they labor in vain who build it.*
                                            —PS. 127:1

It takes many loving hands to build security into your child's life. What a joy to know that you don't labor alone!

One the best ways to garner the support of many helping hands in raising a child is to commit him or her to the care and keeping of God's people.

Parents can do this through a children's dedication service in God's house, the church. Often the pastor will lay his hands on a child and bless the child, a picture of the desire the parents and the entire congregation have in blessing the little one with the best future possible.

In one church, the pastor takes the child and walks up and down the aisle. Sight of the infant often brings smiles to the faces in the congregation.

This is more than a sentimental gesture. In years to come, this church family may literally help raise a child who may unexpectedly lose a parent through death or divorce. Sunday school teachers, youth pastors, and caring adults can be extended family to our children, encircling our immediate families with extra love.

*Thank You, Lord, for all the loving hands at church that bless my children. How can I encourage someone else's child in my church family?*

*There is hope in your future, says the LORD.*
—JER. 31:17

We all grow up with mental pictures of what we will do with our lives. We are either told, "You are a bum; you'll never amount to anything," or "Shoot for the moon; you can do whatever you want."

Words paint pictures: they either box you in or open vast possibilities. In 1970, when Andrea graduated from college, she was told that English literature graduates were unemployable. She'd never land a job. As it happened, Andrea traveled around the world because her parents, wanting to broaden her vision, sent her on a shipboard university. Later, she and her husband lived abroad where she began to write.

After writing six books, she had a family and God broadened her vision farther. As new doors of opportunity opened, she began counseling and teaching as well as writing and mothering.

When her children speculate about what they'll be when they grow up, she says, "Wonderful! And I'm sure you'll do many things you haven't even dreamed of yet."

*Challenge your children to think big!*

*For God so loved the world. . . .*
—JOHN 3:16

The little Bolivian girl with plaintive eyes, a dirt-smudged face, and threadbare dress looked misplaced staring out of a postcard that sat on a middle-class kitchen table. The Indian child lived high in the Andes mountains.

"My dear Stephanie," wrote Mary Anne, a missionary friend of the family's, "I was captured in heart by this small girl, not much younger than you, but so poor, in need of good food, a school, and health care. Perhaps one day you can come and see for yourself and in some way reach out across the bridge of friendship."

Amy, like Stephanie, had friends from other countries. She was used to seeing African faces around the table for dinner every now and then. Her mother went frequently to Africa and shared with Amy her concern for the poor. Amy had organized a hunger drive at school, and now some of the older children were teaching students in the younger grades about hunger awareness.

Stephanie and Amy both had global perspectives because their parents and friends had brought close a world of possibilities.

*Lord, help me to broaden my children's vision to think beyond their own backyard.*

## *May 28* – A PURPOSE AND A PLAN

*All the days ordained for me were written in your book before one of them came to be.*
—PS. 139:16 NIV

God has a purpose and plan for each child's life. His vision for our children is broader and more far-reaching than anything we can ever imagine. In His perfect wisdom, He knows what is best for them and He desires their best.

As students of our children, we can learn what their talents and abilities are and encourage those. We can also work to strengthen their weaknesses. The wisest thing we can do, however, is draw into close partnership with God to raise our children according to His purpose and plan for them. Little by little, step by step, His plan will be revealed.

Regardless of what the future holds, our children will leave home with high worth if we teach them their identity in Christ. The Bible says that His children are deeply loved, highly treasured, of great worth, only a little lower than the angels, secure in His love, made in His image, of more value than the birds of the air, and so important God gave up His only Son to reclaim them from darkness.

When children know how God views them, their future is hope-filled and blessed.

---

*Lord, what is in Your heart for my child? I want to draw close and listen.*

*Behold, I am with you and will keep you wherever you go . . . ; for I will not leave you until I have done what I have spoken to you.* —GEN. 28:15

The blessing can be given in a moment, but in order to carry real meaning, the words must be backed by a commitment to see that it comes to pass. This may take years, and sometimes a lifetime.

God met Jacob on the run—when Jacob was not feeling very noble. He had just tricked his brother, Esau, out of his birthright and was separated from the family, lonely and afraid. In a dream, God assured Jacob of the blessing spoken to his grandfather and father and now to him. The blessing still stood. God's faith in Jacob always left the door open for him to become the man of stature God envisioned him to be.

To see those we love develop their best qualities and talents takes time, energy, and resources on our part. More than that, it takes strong faith in a limitless, infinite God backing us up when we fail and make mistakes.

God is committed to us and He will back up our commitment to others.

*Lord, thank You that You're committed to me. Help me to bless others with my commitment to them.*

> *Thus also faith by itself, if it does not have works,*
> *is dead.*
> —JAMES 2:17

Ongoing, active commitment is the responsibility that goes with giving the blessing. You can affirm someone with words and loving touch, let them know that you value them, and even picture a special future for them, but if those elements of the blessing are not reinforced by actions, they are empty promises.

As James suggested, we need to walk our talk. If you tell your daughter she is talented musically, but don't provide an instrument or lessons, your message is undermined. If a husband encourages his wife to go back to work, but is unwilling to pay for college expenses and help with household chores, how can she feel she really has his blessing?

A tennis pro will tell you that a successful swing depends on follow-through, swinging through on a ball completely, from start to finish. A successful blessing is achieved in the same way—by following through from words of blessing to concrete actions that will make those words come true.

---

*Strengthen my follow-through, Lord, as I bless others.*

*I have confidence in you.*
—GAL. 5:10

Have you ever been in an athletic event and really strained to do your best? What difference did it make to have friends and family cheering you on? To children it makes all the difference in the world. One of the best ways we can affirm our children is through involvement in their activities—even if it is just support from the sidelines.

"My dad never attended one of my little league baseball games in five years," said Jim sadly. "He was too busy." Like many workaholic parents, Jim's father was a shadow figure who worked hard to provide material blessings for his family, but neglected to provide what Jim wanted most: a dad who was there for him as a fan and friend.

Dotty's memories were different. "When my sister and I played basketball in high school, my father attended every game. I was so proud that he was watching," says this outgoing and boisterous eighty-year-old. Knowing how much that meant to her, Dotty loves to sit in the stands and root for her grandsons now. "I wouldn't miss a game," she says.

*What difference does it make to have someone cheer you on? All the difference in the world.*

*God sets the solitary in families.*
—PS. 68:6

Have you ever seen a breathtaking sunset and wished you could share it with someone else? When our hearts are moved by a sunset, a symphony, something humorous, our natural inclination is to turn to someone else to share the discovery, or pleasure. Sharing increases our pleasure and deepens our joy.

This is one reason God put us in families. Judy took her sister and brother-in-law for a bike ride around a city lake. Susan and Mike had left their two boys with the grandparents for a few days. Judy, who didn't have children, thought Susan and Mike would feel relieved to be free of childcare—but she began to wonder.

"I wish Christopher were here," Mike sighed. "Wouldn't he love the lake?" Later, licking a double scoop chocolate ice cream cone, Susan said, "Wouldn't Tim's eyes get big if he saw the size of this cone! It would be so much fun if the boys were here."

Doing things together doubles the fun and provides family memories that serve as a touchstone of closeness throughout the years.

*Is there something our whole family could do together today, Lord?*

*Practice hospitality.*
—ROM. 12:13 NIV

We can demonstrate active commitment to our children not only by sharing in their activities, but also including them in ours.

One of Rob's favorite photographs shows him, at eight years old, proudly holding up a ten-pound snapper caught off the coast of Florida. Finally, Rob was old enough to go with his dad on one of his many business trips. After the business part of the trip, Rob and his dad relaxed with some men on a fishing boat. Rob had the time of his life just going along as one of the boys.

Our children spend most of their time removed from the daily activities of our lives. Have your children ever seen your office, if you work outside the home? Have they met your friends? Do they take part in your leisure activities?

Nothing can make your children feel more valuable than sharing your world with them. Ask them to help make dinner (even though it may take twice as long!) or invite them to the office to see your new project.

*How can I invite companionship with my children today?*

*The LORD will bless his people with peace.*
—PS. 29:11

Jan couldn't rest until each item was scratched off her to-do list, but the list seemed endless. She felt tyrannized by little things.

"Pick up something at the grocery store, make a deposit, drop off film . . ." As Jan was working on her list, her five-year-old noticed that they had just passed a park and it was a lovely summer day. Her daughter begged to stop at the park after their errands were done.

"Sure," said Jan, making a decision to put an immediate halt to the tyranny of little things. "That sounds like a great idea!"

So Jan and Cassie took a breather. They sipped juice boxes in the sunshine, played on the swings and talked about happy memories. "Remember the time when . . ."

Jan felt much more rested, looking at the sunlight glimmering on a nearby lake and listening to Cassie's laughter. This peace she knew was a blessing from God—a time set aside to just enjoy her daughter and God's good creation. But in order to receive that blessing, she needed to be committed to making it happen.

*Active commitment is a daily choice.*

*He grants the barren woman a home, like a joyful mother of children.* —PS. 113:9

God's vision for a mother is joy. She is a woman no longer alone, but needed by others and needing others. A mother belongs to a family, surrounded by those she loves; yet stay-at-home moms in our society are ridiculed. So many moms walk out.

Some moms literally leave, seduced by a romantic affair or visions of a new career. Then there are those who stay at home, but their hearts are elsewhere: organizing church activities or community fundraisers.

Sally was the latter kind of mom. There were so many hurting people at church she couldn't ignore them. Eventually, however, she began to realize that she poured so much of herself out for other people she had nothing left to give her own family. She was exhausted at the end of a day of giving.

Sally was noticing that her children were acting out in anger and rebellion because of her lack of attention. Her house was not the joyous place she wanted it to be. She began to cut back on outside commitments and prayed, "Lord, help me to keep the best alabaster flask of affection for You and my family."

*Lord, I need to cut back on outside commitments. Show me how.*

> *To everything there is a season, a time for every*
> *purpose under heaven.*                         —ECCL. 3:1

Being actively committed to our children takes time. Our sons and daughters are only loaned to us for a season. Soon they are grown and gone.

"I wish Dad would retire," moaned a little girl. "Then he could play with me."

Another little boy rarely saw his father. The busy executive, who usually spent Saturdays at the office, sat down to read the paper at the kitchen table. His son was overjoyed to find him at home. He ran upstairs, emptied his piggy bank, and came back down to the kitchen. He stood quietly by his dad waiting for him to look up from the paper.

"Well, what do you want?" his father asked, perturbed.

The little boy held out a handful of bills and change. "Dad, this is all I have, eight dollars and sixty-four cents. I will give it all to you if you play with me today."

The years pass quickly. We need to take every opportunity to bless our children by spending time with them because that opportunity won't be there forever.

*Father, forgive me when my children have to beg for my time. Today I will give it to them freely.*

*I will not leave you orphans.*
—JOHN 14:18

A child's deepest fear is of being abandoned by his parents. "If you go jogging, you have to go fast," said a four-year-old, "because your mommy and daddy might run ahead of you and leave you."

In our fast-paced world, our children do have to run fast to keep up with us and sometimes they can't run fast enough. Their parents' attention always seems out of reach.

Helen was an attentive mom—most of the time. But when she went shopping, she would sometimes wander down an aisle, leaving her preschooler in another aisle. She wasn't that far away, but her little girl, who suddenly felt afraid and overwhelmed by the bigness of the store and the busy crowds, would break down in sobs, feeling abandoned. "Someday I'm going to get bigger and leave you behind," she said indignantly.

It finally dawned on Helen how insensitive she had been of her daughter's feelings. Active commitment means being emotionally present to our children as well as being physically there for them.

*Help me regard my child's feelings, Lord, as highly as I do my own.*

*For where your treasure is, there your heart will be also.*
—MATT. 6:21

Our children know what we treasure, for that is where we invest our passion, our time, our resources. It is that to which we are wholeheartedly committed.

What does wholehearted commitment to a child look like and what difference does it make? When I (Gary) think of that question, I immediately think of an experience in high school. Math was a subject I hated and never did well in. I knew immediately I was going to flunk geometry, my senior year of high school, because my teacher told me. To reinforce this, the half of the class that was failing sat in the back of the room.

One day everything changed. We were assigned a new teacher. "If anyone fails this class, I have failed," he said. He pledged to do whatever he could to see that we all passed the course. This meant staying after school to tutor us and helping with homework on weekends. After homework sessions, he even played a little volleyball with us for fun.

The turnaround in that class was dramatic. Everyone passed! That dedicated teacher motivated me so much, I not only got an A in the class, but ended up minoring in math in college!

*Think of the pay-offs an investment in your children can make.*

*O LORD, You have searched me and known me. . . .*
*and are acquainted with all my ways.*
—PS. 139:1, 3

We need to spend time with our children not only to show we value them, but also to get to know them. Scripture tells us that Jacob blessed his children with a blessing uniquely suited to each one. The better we know each child's needs and interests, the better we can bless them.

To do this we need to become students of those we wish to bless. This is something I (John) have seen modeled for me all my life. In my mom's home is a bookshelf filled with seemingly unrelated books. However, to my two brothers and me they have great significance.

One shelf is filled with books on theology and psychology, the subjects that interest me most. Another shelf is filled with books on genetics and medical journals, which reflect my twin brother's interests. The third shelf holds books on operating road construction equipment. She has read these to better converse with us in our fields of interest.

Mom's bookshelf speaks volumes about her commitment to try to understand and communicate with each of her three sons.

---

*I will learn something new about each of my children today.*

> *Ask, and it will be given to you; seek, and you will find; knock, and it will be opened to you.*
>
> —MATT. 7:7

How can we get to know our children? One thing that helps is to be lovingly persistent in communicating with them. I (Gary) learned this in a surprising way when I was on a TV talk show with my son Greg.

Greg was on the show to share his perspective on parent/child communication. The show's host asked Greg what he would urge parents to do to better communicate with their children. Greg answered, "Don't believe it when your son or daughter tells you they don't want to talk. Sometimes I'll say that to my dad and mom when they ask me how I'm doing, but I don't mean it. I'm really hoping they will be persistent and help me talk about it."

If we continue to knock gently on the door of our children's hearts, looking for times when meaningful communication can take place, they will eventually let us into the inner room of their thoughts and feelings.

Driving in the car, taking a walk, or dropping into a hamburger place all provide a relaxed environment where children may find it easy to talk about what's on their minds.

---

*Lord, help me to look for moments when my child wants to share his heart.*

*The heart of the prudent acquires knowledge, and
the ear of the wise seeks knowledge.*
—PROV. 18:15

Alison dashed in the door. "Hey, Mom, I got a goal!"

"Wonderful." Her mom smiled, as Alison hopped up
in her lap.

Jan hadn't been able to go to the soccer game that
day and Alison was eager to give her the play-by-play
account of her achievement.

"Did Dad say he was proud of you?" Jan asked.

"No." The excitement drained out of Alison's voice.
"He never thinks anything I do is good enough."

Jan talked to her husband later about the importance of affirmation. Ross was a great dad, but one of
his blind spots was forgetting to praise his children. His
parents had not verbally praised him, so affirmation
was a parenting skill he needed to acquire.

Jan had her blind spots too. Her parents had been
weak on firm, consistent discipline. She needed to become a stronger disciplinarian. "Say it once," Ross
would remind her. None of us is a perfect parent, but
we can be wiser and more effective by listening to the
advice of a supportive spouse or friend.

*How wonderful to know I don't parent alone!*

## June 11 – LISTEN TO OTHERS

> *Without counsel, plans go awry, but in the*
> *multitude of counselors they are established.*
> —PROV. 15:22

Another way to learn about our children is to listen to others who know them well—teachers, scout leaders, coaches, other parents who observe them.

At a preschool conference, the teacher asked if Gretchen's daughter had an older sibling.

The teacher said that at times Kari could be disruptive. She thought this might be a reason. She had noticed that younger siblings frequently fight to get ahead in lines and are more demanding. At home, they often feel overlooked. They don't want to be slighted at school either.

Kari's teacher had found that if she touched Kari lightly on the shoulder to acknowledge her, while firmly telling her to wait her turn in class, Kari would patiently wait until being called on. She also suggested letting Kari participate in more family decision-making at home to let her know she was valued as much as her older sister.

This advice gave Gretchen new insights. She began to use both of these suggestions to bless Kari and let her know how special she was.

*As a student of my child, Lord, I am so grateful to have many teachers.*

*Therefore be followers of God as dear children.*
*And walk in love as Christ also has loved us.*
—EPH. 5:1–2

Active commitment also involves discipline—molding and shaping our children's character to bring out the best in them so they can be a blessing to themselves and others. This sometimes requires the greatest investment on our part.

Children learn by example. The best way to inspire obedience in them is to model Christlike behavior ourselves and let our children know that we are accountable to God just as they are.

When Brian and his brother were small, there was a time when they fought like cats and dogs. Brian's father asked why he and his brother always got into skirmishes. "You and Mommy do it, why can't we?" Brian retorted. Brian's parents, though dedicated Christians, had had no idea their arguments had such an impact on their children.

"The next time you see your mother and me fighting," said Brian's dad, "I'll give you a dollar." At the first sound of dissension, Brian was there with his hand out. His father paid him, but only once. After that, the fighting subsided between Brian's parents and, in turn, between Brian and his brother.

*Lord, help me to hold myself accountable to walk in love even as I ask my children to.*

*And you, fathers, do not provoke your children to
wrath, but bring them up in the training and
admonition of the Lord.*
                                                —EPH. 6:4

Parents often find themselves motivating their children by coercion, threats, manipulation, and anger. Scripture says this is not the way to bring up children. To "train" suggests inspiring cooperation, not evoking a tug of war.

Small children often feel frustrated because our demands seem overwhelming. For example, if you tell a four-year-old to clean his room, he will look overwhelmed. Breaking the job down into bite-size pieces—fold three shirts, then put the crayons in the bucket—makes cleaning up his bedroom more manageable.

Chores are more fun if turned into games. To get a preschooler to help empty the trash, one mom pretended she was Oscar the Grouch going on a trash hunt. The mom poured the trash into her bag, which her daughter opened and shut like Oscar's mouth. "Yum, yum, yum." The preschooler giggled, imitating the lovable puppet.

Being heavy-handed is not a very effective motivator. It crushes the one being badgered. There is a better way, Jesus said. The way of love.

*Lord, give me creativity and care in training my children.*

*Apply your heart to instruction.*
—PROV. 23:12

Creative parents not only use the intellect to teach, but also the heart. One of the best ways to reach a child's heart is to use visual input, along with words.

One mother used her microwave oven to teach her son about anger. She took a clear plastic mug, filled it with water and turned the oven on high. She compared the boiling water to his emotions when he got angry. Just as she could push the pause button to stop the oven before the water boiled over, he could stop to talk to her so she could help him with his frustrations before his emotions boiled over.

Another mom used a proverb to motivate her son to get to work. She was inspired by Proverbs 6:6, "Go to the ant, you sluggard! Consider her ways." This mom bought her son an ant farm which provided living examples of the traits she wanted to build into her son. He was fascinated watching the insects' non-stop activity as they worked together to accomplish different tasks.

One day his mom talked to him about how he could be a better ant helping around the house and doing schoolwork. She noticed immediate changes in his behavior!

*Lord, help me to aim for my child's heart as well as his mind when I teach.*

## June 15 – GETTING THE PICTURE

> *A fool despises his father's instruction, but he who receives reproof is prudent.*          —PROV. 15:5

When my (Gary's) son Michael was thirteen, I needed to talk to him about eating too much junk food. Lectures went over like a lead balloon. Then I tried a word picture.

Tapping into a major interest of his, golfing, provided the inroad to his heart that I needed. Mike was excited when I suggested we go golfing one afternoon. As we played, I noticed that he kept slicing the ball.

"If Jack Nicklaus were playing with us today," I said, "would you listen to him if he explained how you could get rid of your slice?"

"You bet I would!"

I told Mike that in one area of his life, I saw him doing something that was like slicing every shot into the woods. Medical experts, just as knowledgeable about good eating habits as Jack Nicklaus was about golf, said that eating too much junk food was unhealthy. Ignoring their warning was like having Jack Nicklaus tell you how to improve your swing, then refusing to take his advice.

Michael got the picture, and gradually his junk-food diet became a thing of the past.

---

*A word picture is worth a thousand lectures.*

*The LORD repay your work, and a full reward be
given you.*
                                    —RUTH 2:12

One of the most loving ways to motivate children is
to reinforce their good behavior through rewards.

Parents are paid for their work. Why shouldn't children have a full reward for their contribution to the
family? Having a "chip jar" works well for young children. They can decorate construction-paper coins and
write their names on a bank-jar. Twenty chips can
earn a treat, a special outing or a dollar; whatever reward they choose from your designated selection.

As they get older, you can reward chips, not only
for chores, but for attitudes you want to instill in your
children. For example, give a cooperative chip for
minding right away or a peace-making chip to a sibling
who resolves an argument.

Let children keep track of their own chips or mark
a chart to measure progress—whatever it takes to give
them hands-on involvement in the process. A system
of rewards that children understand and can manage
gives them pride in their accomplishments and underscores how important they are to the family.

*I like to be rewarded for my work. Lord, help me to share that plea-
sure with my children.*

> *But let your "Yes" be "Yes," and your "No," "No."*
> —MATT. 5:37

A familiar sight in the grocery store is Mom or Dad pushing a cart while a little one begs for something he can't have. "No," the parent says firmly. The child persists, pleading, nagging, droning on. "No, no, no, no, no!" says the parent, until they reach the check-out stand. Finally, the beleaguered parent gives in, "Oh, all right."

An inconsistent parent produces an inconsistent child. Can you hear that same child when, years later, he is approached by a friend who coaxes him to try alcohol or drugs? "Just once," says his friend. The child firmly declines because he knows it is wrong. "No, no, no, no . . ." then finally gives in, "Oh, all right."

In a day of situational ethics, the Bible's insistence on absolutes may seem old-fashioned, but it makes sense in child-rearing. The goal of discipline is to produce an individual who can discipline himself one day. Stick-to-your-guns consistency in parenting provides a child with security and the strength to someday stand firm on his own.

*Lord, give me the strength to say no to my inconsistency.*

*Do not withhold correction from a child.*
—PROV. 23:13

What happens if we neglect to discipline our children? When Mary needed to leave the house, her husband agreed to watch their three small children. "No problem," he said. Mary left her husband on the couch, comfortably reading a magazine.

When she came home, she found him in the same spot. "How did it go?" she asked. Jack smiled and said they were quiet as mice.

They were quiet; quiet as busy mice. While Jack was absorbed in his magazine, the children had covered one wall of the house with crayons and paint!

Jack and Mary could look back at that incident and laugh, but as children grow older the consequence of neglect is no laughing matter. Children need correction.

A permissive father sat in our office, crying because he had just found out that his sixteen-year-old daughter was on drugs and pregnant from a relationship with a twenty-six-year-old, divorced man. He told us, "We didn't want her to date him, but what could we say?"

*Adults as well as children need to learn to say no.*

> *Great is our Lord . . . ; His understanding is infinite.*
> —PS. 147:5

While helping our children remain anchored, we need to remain anchored in God's love ourselves.

Imagine a mother's surprise as her baby, who once looked up into her eyes with adoration, now becomes an angry eight-year-old. No longer a lamb, her eyes reflect tiger fierceness.

Even the most understanding mother can feel attacked. Laurie, ripping at her hair in the morning, unhappy with the way it looks, screams at her mother, "I hate you," while also sobbing, "Mommy, Mommy." That ambivalence of emotions sends them both into a turmoil.

Mom knows that beneath the rage is a little girl who cannot articulate her feelings and is crying for help even while rejecting the one she loves most. Mom also knows better than to take those angry words personally, but sometimes she lets the anger strip her affection away. Gone is the understanding; her cup of mercy has run dry.

Then suddenly, Mom remembers the times she has been a little child, screaming at God in anger, all the while needing His comfort. She remembers the times she was forgiven when she didn't deserve forgiveness. Her cup of mercy, so small, is refilled with a vast ocean of love.

---

*Father, today I will draw on Your abundant mercy as I meet situations of anger.*

*He brought me out into a spacious place; he*
*rescued me because he delighted in me.*
—PS. 18:19 NIV

Don't bug me!" shouted Katie when her mother asked her for the umpteenth time if she had done her homework.

It wasn't just homework. It was the way she wore her hair, the friends she kept, the magazines she read. Katie felt like her mother was always looking over her shoulder, telling her what to do and what not to do. Katie felt backed into a corner, trapped.

That is how David felt when he wrote today's verse. His enemies were backing him into a corner. Then the Lord provided a way out, leading him to "a spacious place" where he could relax and feel safe.

We bless our children when we give them space. We can do this by: standing back and letting them be free to express themselves (if it is not injurious to themselves or others), allowing them to fail and learn from their mistakes, granting them more responsibility not less, showing them that we delight in who they are and what they are becoming.

*Am I my child's worst enemy or best friend?*

*The fear of the LORD is the instruction of wisdom,
and before honor is humility.*     —PROV. 15:33

One of the hardest things for most parents to do is to admit their mistakes to a child. In the Scriptures, however, the humble readily admit they don't know it all. It increases our children's self-worth if they see us as open, teachable and willing to be corrected.

I learned this during a conversation with my (Gary's) daughter, Kari. Kari had been studying several chapters of Proverbs in her college Bible class. She asked me to read them with her. As we read, we evaluated our daily actions in light of what the Bible said.

Kari read one verse and suggested that it was an area I needed to work on. After she made the comment, I could tell that she didn't know whether she should have said it. She looked at me to see if I was upset or if she was in trouble!

When she saw I was open and accepting to correction—especially from her—it helped her be more open toward things she needed to work on in her own life.

After that talk, we grew in respect for each other because we could both admit that at times we needed correction like everyone else.

*Humility is the mark of maturity as a parent.*

*We know that all things work together for good to those who love God.* —ROM. 8:28

Being actively committed to our children means helping them see the hidden blessings that can emerge from the worst of trials.

When problems come, children often look to their parents to see how they respond. Do you panic? "Oh, no, now what are we going to do!" Do you lecture your child? "You have embarrassed me." Do you become overly pious? "You're going to grow spiritually through this!"

A more constructive approach is to find the value in trials. I (Gary) ask my children this question, "Would you like to spend some time this week unwrapping the trial you've received?" It may take days or weeks after the event before they are ready to do this, but when they are ready, it is such an opportunity to teach them about the depth of God's grace.

Troubled times can bring loved ones closer. They can help us grow in compassion and humility. They can be a catalyst to inspire us to reach out to others in need.

*When my child meets a storm in life, we will search beyond tears to find treasure.*

> *He will teach us His ways.*
> —MIC. 4:2

Sometimes pain provides an opportunity a parent has been looking for to teach a valuable lesson. When a child is hurting, he is often open and ready to listen. This poem, "Antidote to Anger," captures such a teachable moment:

> *I was playing outside*
> *When she called me a name*
> *I got mad, I mean really mad,*
> *So I came home and told you,*
> *And you sat down and spoke to me of*
> *Anger, the anger that was suffocating*
> *All the beauty, truth and reason in my life.*
> *At that moment, Anger, Like a fishbone*
> *Stuck coarsely in my throat.*
> *You talked and gave me calm and comfort.*
> *And you taught me a forever lesson.*
> *From you I learned that*
> *Only love removes my anger*
> *In a safe and painless way.*
> —SOURCE UNKNOWN

*Lord, help to be aware of moments when I can teach my child forever lessons.*

*The body is sown in corruption, it is raised in incorruption. It is sown in dishonor, it is raised in glory. It is sown in weakness, it is raised in power.*
—1 COR. 15:42–43

Some truths we teach our children are too deep for words. One father wanted to teach his children what a loving and powerful God they had even in the midst of grief—after their one remaining grandparent died. He did this by giving his children a living example of how God could turn tragedy into triumph.

On a Saturday morning, he gathered his children together and let them each plant a sweet pea seed in a little container of potting soil. While they were having fun planting and watering, he explained that even though their grandmother's physical body had been placed in the ground, one day God would raise it up, imperishable, in a new and beautiful form as glorious as any flower.

These words seemed to bounce off one son who was still struggling. He remained angry and sullen—until the first sprouts of green shot up from his planting. That's when his father's words sank in. As this little boy saw God's incredible power to bring new life, he let go of his anger and was able to move beyond his sadness.

---

*The world around us is a wonderful classroom.*

> *And He said to me, "My grace is sufficient for you,*
> *for My strength is made perfect in weakness."*
> —2 COR. 12:9

Sometimes the active commitment that some of our loved ones require is almost impossible to give. Yet God is faithful to provide the strength we need.

"I had always dreamed of owning a beautiful vase," said a young woman discussing what it was like to become the mother of a handicapped child. "Instead of the work of art I'd seen in my mind for so long, I was given a vase that was shattered into a thousand pieces. My heart was broken into as many pieces, and I cried long after my tears had run dry.

"Little by little, the pile of pieces took shape. As the days went by, I gathered more love and patience to glue them together than I ever thought possible. In time, I began to see a masterpiece growing from what had been a mess.

"My husband and I asked God to give us a special love for our daughter, and He has. Of course, there are days when I tire of picking up the pieces. But somehow, the work is easier now. So much love and commitment have already gone into cementing her life together that I can't imagine loving anyone or anything more."

*Give me grace, Lord. Give me grace to go on.*

*His faithfulness continues through all generations.*
—PSALM 100:5 NIV

Being actively committed to our children doesn't stop when they are grown. We can still be there to bless them. When Jane was young, her mom always prayed for her as she went out the door to school. "I'll be praying about that paper you're writing."

Years later Jane was no longer writing school essays, but national magazine articles. She was accustomed to interviewing celebrities and writing major stories, but there were still times when she fell apart. On those days, it meant a lot to get a phone call from her mom. "What are you working on today, honey? How can I pray for you?"

"I'm interviewing Neville Marriner, Mom. I only have twenty minutes before his ten o'clock performance to get the story and photos. I don't know how I'm going to do it."

"You'll make it," her mother assured her. "Just remember you are doing what you love most in the world."

As Jane rushed to the concert hall that morning, she felt nervous. Suddenly she remembered her mother's words, "You're doing what you love most in the world." Jane smiled and decided to enjoy herself.

*Lord, help me never to stop blessing my children.*

> *And whatever you do, do it heartily, as to the Lord*
> *and not to men.*
> —COL. 3:23

Sometimes, as adults, children need their parents' help even more. Mom and Dad continue to play a blessing role as they provide ways for their children to realize their potential.

Lisa came from a strong Christian home that held up the ideals of Christian service, but it wasn't until she was forty that she became interested in ministry. With two children to raise, she couldn't afford the time or expense to go to seminary, so she decided to attend seminars for training. One seminar really caught her interest, but it was out-of-state and she couldn't afford to travel there.

How surprised she was to open a letter from her parents one day. "Dear Lisa," it began, "this is a note to let you know that we have selected you to be our *Missionary of the Month.* Please accept the enclosed check from our family missionary fund to be used for your seminar expenses. We love you! It's a wonderful encouragement to us to see you carry on the Lord's work."

Lisa was touched, not only by their financial support, but also by their words that showed they valued what mattered most to her.

*Lord, thank You for the blessing of my parents. How can I bless them today?*

*Be kind to one another, tenderhearted, forgiving
one another, just as God in Christ also forgave you.*
—EPH. 4:32

Just as parents continue to bless their children, children should bless their parents to return, in some small measure, the love they've been shown.

Weddings have a way of bringing back memories—pleasant and painful. As Leanne danced with her father-in-law, she noticed that his eyes got soft, almost sad. Frank, a man of few words, could not easily express his feelings. What he said next must have been difficult to say.

Celebrating his youngest son's wedding brought a deep regret that he had not attended the wedding of his older son, Leanne's husband. Frank wanted her to know that he was sorry. Then, what he really wanted to know, but could not express is, could she forgive him?

Leanne loved her husband's father. And she was surprised that after twenty years, this still bothered him. "Frank," she smiled, glad to have a chance to express her appreciation for him, "it doesn't matter at all. You and Gwen have done so many wonderful things for John and me through the years, we couldn't feel more loved than we do."

*One way to bless our parents is to forgive past mistakes and assure them of our love.*

> *With the LORD there is mercy, and with Him is*
> *abundant redemption.*
> —PS. 130:7

If you received the blessing from your parents, you will find it easier to give the blessing. But many of us, even though we understand how to give the blessing and earnestly want to put it into practice, will find it difficult if we have never seen it modeled for us. We may feel awkward trying to develop new patterns of relating as a parent if we grew up in homes that withheld the blessing.

However, God is in the business of transforming our lives, making old things new. In the coming days we'll see how men and women who grew up without the blessing learned to reclaim it.

Like me (John), you may be someone who grew up in a home that bestowed part of the blessing, but not all of it. In my home I heard lots of warm, affirming words. But hugging and touching were not part of the way we expressed love and acceptance. When I married and had children, I found it easy to verbally praise my family. Because I understood the importance of meaningful touch I wanted to reinforce my words with a hug. It was awkward and unnatural at first, but I slowly trained myself to be more affectionate.

*God blesses us as we reach out to others. The changes will come.*

*He . . . took her by the hand and called, saying,*
*"Little girl, arise."*
                                        —LUKE 8:54

Touch communicates warmth and affirmation. Without it, it is hard for a child to feel loved and highly valued. The good news is that even though our parents may not have been able to communicate unconditional love through meaningful touch, God can do it through other people in our lives.

Mary Jo and Jan were both single moms. One day at lunch, Jan reached over and stroked Mary Jo's cheek when Mary Jo was feeling low. She did it casually, almost jokingly. "There, there," said Jan as if she were speaking to a little girl, "everything is going to be all right."

Mary Jo told her friend later, "You know, that felt good."

That day it dawned on them that they, women who had been deprived of loving touch as children, could offer each other safe, nurturing touches that could help restore their touch deficit. They became nurturing buddies. Along with reassuring touches, they affirmed each other with words and occasional gifts.

---

*Loving touch can bring new life.*

*He now showed them the full extent of his love. He poured water into a basin and began to wash his disciples' feet.*
                                        **—JOHN 13:1, 4 NIV**

Mary's father had never affirmed and blessed her. Like so many daughters who develop "father hunger," she tried to satisfy that deep need for affection in the arms of many men. Finally, she found one man who truly loved her.

Mary told Steve about her past, but it did not lessen his love for her. He still wanted to marry her. Even though Mary knew that Steve had forgiven her and he assured her that God had forgiven her, too, she still tormented herself with guilt.

On their wedding night, Steve wanted to show his new bride the full extent of his love. He wanted her to know, really know, how highly he valued her. So he filled a basin with warm water, took a towel and knelt at Mary's feet. As he tenderly washed her feet, tears flooded down Mary's cheeks. Steve wrapped his arms around her and let her sob out years of pain.

That was six years ago. Mary tells the story, still amazed that those old feelings of guilt and unworthiness have never returned. It was as if Jesus Himself had washed her feet with His tears and restored her with His embrace.

------

*Sometimes touch can release hurt that words can't.*

*How sweet are Your words to my taste.*
—PS. 119:103

A parent's bitter words can leave their sting long after the child is grown and gone from home.

When Nancy's boss at work made a casual comment, "Hey, Nancy, why didn't you take that shift off? That was dumb," Nancy felt her body shake and her palms get sweaty. Just hearing the word *dumb*, flooded Nancy with shameful feelings. She had been raised in a family of three daughters by a father who devalued women. "You are just a bunch of dumb broads!" her father would shout.

Fortunately, Nancy married a Christian man who knew how to verbally express high value to her. Matt's words of affection and praise were a great source of blessing. "I have full confidence in you," he would say as she tackled something difficult. Matt knew that Nancy was sensitive about never having gone to college while he had a degree. He would affirm her practical side, by saying "Sometimes I think you know more than I."

"Matt is my blessing," says Nancy.

*Affirming words can sweeten a bitter past.*

*Then a voice came from heaven, "You are My
beloved Son, in whom I am well pleased."*
—MARK 1:11

Dick never heard his father praise him. Instead, he
grew up with angry put-downs that stung like slaps to
the face, "You'll never amount to anything," "You're
worthless." "Knucklehead" and "dummy" were considered affectionate terms.

Abuse tends to repeat itself: an angry grandfather
degrades a father who in turn puts down his son. Dick
wanted to stop the cycle of verbal abuse in his generation and turn it around.

As a Christian, Dick discovered that he did not have
to mindlessly continue his family's destructive patterns. As he heard the heavenly Father's voice in Scripture and learned to personalize it, "Dick, *you* are my
beloved son in whom I am well pleased," he began to
distance himself from the internal tapes he had grown
up with. Gradually they lost their power over him.

Out of the affirmation Dick was receiving grew a
desire to speak loving words to his own son. Even as a
baby, before his son could understand his words, Dick
would put a gentle hand on the little boy's head and
speak these words in prayer, "You are my beloved son,
in whom I am well pleased."

*Lord, help me to hear Your words of affirmation and let them trans-
form my inner woundedness.*

*The LORD is merciful and gracious, slow to anger, and abounding in mercy.*                                    —PS. 103:8

My dad was a Type A person," said Penny. "He would stomp into the house after work with a red face. I knew to get out of the way because his anger was explosive. Whatever I did made him mad."

When Penny became a mother, she found she was impatient like her father and a yeller. Penny didn't want to repeat her father's destructive parenting style. When she lost her temper and yelled at her four-year-old, she asked him to pray for her. "Dear Jesus," he would say, "please help my Mommy to calm down."

Penny's tendency was to be abrupt, "Andrew, stop that, right now!" But by watching the teachers at pre-school, she learned how to creatively get attention. "Andrew, freeze like a popsicle. What color are you?"

And when anger got the better of her, she apologized. "Andrew, Mommy was wrong. Can we start over?"

Following his mother's lead, Andrew sometimes would say, "Mommy, I shouldn't have done that. Can we start over?"

Together, they were learning.

*When I'm angry today, I'll apologize and start over.*

*Set a guard, O Lord, over my mouth; keep watch over the door of my lips.* —PS. 141:3

Angry dads can bring cursing instead of blessing into a home, moms too must watch their words. It is common for divorced moms who feel abandoned by their husbands to bad-mouth the missing spouse. This not only robs their children of blessing words, but makes bitterness a poison to their own hearts.

How can we focus on the positive with our words? Sometimes it helps to have someone else to keep us accountable. Jane and Pam were divorcées who had friends who were also divorced. They noticed that many of their friends were stuck in the past, re-living hurt from as long ago as twenty years. After spending time with these bitter buddies, they went away hating every man they saw!

To keep from slipping into the poor-me syndrome themselves, they made a pact to help each other stay focused on the positive. When they felt fed up, they would call each other and have a whining session. After they'd gotten their gripes out, they would have a good laugh, letting go of bad feelings and keeping their lives in perspective.

*We need to help each other to bless, not curse.*

*Her worth is far above rubies.*
—PROV. 31:10

Every child should be highly valued, but sometimes parents, who never loved and accepted themselves, cannot esteem their own children. As a result, sons and daughters who live apart from the blessing often feel undervalued and worthless.

"My father never showed us respect or love," said Marie. "He never told us he loved us. If we asked a question, he acted perturbed. Even his body language seemed to show disgust and tell us that we were unworthy of his time or attention."

As an adult, Marie discovered a heavenly Father who restored her sense of worth. Affirming Christian friends also helped build her up. And Marie's husband showed her dignity and respect in gentle, loving ways.

"Bob hugs me and touches me, even when I've been yucky," says Marie. "He treats me wonderfully in front of the children. But it wasn't until the other night when I was with my family, and I saw how my brother and sister still grapple for Dad's attention that I realized the extent of my freedom. It has been a slow process over the years, but I actually feel free of that pain."

*Lord, help me to be patient with the healing process.*

> *Jesus said to them, "Take off the grave clothes and let him go."*
> —JOHN 11:44 NIV

I feel like I'm in a cocoon," said Jen, an attractive middle-aged woman. "I'm not married. I don't have children. I don't have a job."

As tears flooded down her face, Jen confided how sad she felt that she had not been able to live up to her mom's expectations. Her mother was dead, but her expectations still weighed heavily on her. She knew in her mind that her mom had been trying to live out, in her daughter, some of her unfulfilled expectations. She also knew that it wasn't fair, but in her heart it was hard to let go of those demands and simply feel free to live her own life.

Jen felt like Lazarus, imprisoned in a dark tomb. A friend suggested that Jen imagine herself in that Bible story. In prayer, Jen imagined Jesus calling *her* name. Slowly, she walked out of the tomb, not by her own strength, but by His love drawing her into the light. Face to face, she saw how much Jesus loved her. In that moment, her spirit felt released. She saw herself as a butterfly with gorgeous wings—the picture of hope she needed to move out into a new future.

*Let Jesus call you to new life in Him today.*

*I sought the LORD, and He heard me, and delivered me from all my fears.*
                                    —PS. 34:4

Sometimes facing past hurts honestly can bring unexpected results.

Greg was four years old when his parents brought home two beautiful baby girls from the hospital. Greg now had to share his parents' time not with one sister, but two. When people commented on the two cute little girls in the double stroller, they ignored an older brother who also longed for affirmation.

As an adult, Greg attended one of our seminars where he learned about the family blessing. Greg knew his parents loved and accepted him, but he still had a nagging doubt that he was loved as much as his sisters.

Greg knew he needed to deal honestly with his feelings about missing out on part of the blessing. Mustering up all the courage he had, he decided to discuss his concern with his parents.

His mother started to cry. "I've wanted to talk about this for a long time," she said. Sharing their feelings openly, Greg and his parents cried, laughed, and hugged each other, growing closer than they had been in years.

------

*Families are bound up with each other's hurt, but also set free by each other's healing.*

*And you shall know the truth, and the truth shall make you free.*
—JOHN 8:32

Rachel was a woman in her mid-fifties who lived a lonely, isolated life. Her self-esteem was so low she was afraid to invite anyone over for coffee or lunch for fear they'd say no. Rachel had a strong sense of inferiority rooted in childhood: she felt her mother always favored her younger brother and rejected her. No amount of affirmation could change this negative self-perception.

In Rachel's case, this may have been true. But sometimes our perceptions of the past are distorted. Like Rachel, Becky had always felt jealous of her younger sister. One Christmas during a family reunion, Becky decided to spend an evening alone with her sister going over childhood memories. She was surprised to learn that she and her sister had totally different perceptions of the past. In fact, Becky's sister confided, she had always been jealous of her older sister!

"I never knew you felt that way!" Becky and her sister laughed, comparing notes and clearing up their misconceptions. As they shared the truth, they felt free to get to know each other all over again as grown women with much to offer each other.

*Walking in the light of truth dispels the darkness of the past.*

*Show mercy and compassion everyone to his
brother.*
                                              —ZECH. 7:9

If you have missed out on the blessing, you may feel
that you can't go home again and change the past. You
may not be able to change the past, but understanding
it can change your perspective and help you grow in
compassion for your parents.

Andrea had always struggled with how distant her
father was. He was kind. He never raised his voice to
any of the children, but he never expressed affirmation either. Except for the occasional hug, his lack of
touch made Andrea feel she had never received the
blessing.

One day Andrea asked her father about his background. She found out things she never knew about
her dad. As the son of British parents, he had been
taught to address his dad formally as "Sir" and to keep
his distance. Touch was taboo and words of praise
non-existent.

She was surprised to learn that he had worked very
hard to provide blessing for his children that he had
never had. We may discover that our parents need the
blessing from us just as much as (or more than) we
need it from them!

*Lord, give me understanding and compassion as I seek to reclaim
the blessing.*

> *Do not despise your mother when she is old.*
> —PROV. 23:22

Sharon's parents were in their forties when she was born. They were both professionals and had not planned to have another child. Sharon knew she was not wanted. She was treated more like a boarder than a daughter. At thirteen, she lived in a separate apartment and was told to take care of herself.

As an adult, it would have been easy for Sharon to turn her back on her mother. But Sharon became a Christian, married a loving husband, and found healing from her childhood hurts. When she realized how blessed she was, she cried, knowing that her mother had never experienced the unconditional love she now knew. Sharon decided to give her mom the blessing she had missed.

Unlike her other siblings, who despised their mother, Sharon invited her mom into her life. They laughed, did fun things together, became close through phone calls. When Sharon told her mom she was her best friend, her mother was moved to tears.

Sharon says, "I have a real sense that the Lord is opening up channels of communication between me and my mom. He is calling me to be a peacemaker in my family."

*Are you called to be a peacemaker in your family?*

*I cancelled all that debt of yours because you
begged me to. Shouldn't you have had mercy on
your fellow servant just as I had on you?*
—MATT. 18:32–33 NIV

Forgiveness is one of the greatest keys to getting un-
stuck from the past and reclaiming blessing in the future.

Anne's parents started drinking heavily when she
was in junior high school. Her life was one of confu-
sion, anger, pain, and loneliness. In her helplessness,
Anne cried out to God for help—a God she didn't know.

Help came. A neighbor invited Anne to church
where she then came to know Christ. When her parents moved out of town, a church family took her in
and provided the love and acceptance she'd never
known.

Ten years later, Anne's parents, penniless, jobless,
sick, and broken, were released from an institution
into her care. "As I took them into my home," Anne
remembers, "God asked me to forgive and forget all
the hurts my parents had caused me in the past. He
seemed to be saying, 'Can't you forgive them out of
the riches of love and grace I have given you?'" When
Anne totally forgave her parents, she was free to embrace and bless them, as she had been blessed.

*Forgiveness is a decision, not a feeling.*

*You have set my heart free.*
—PS. 119:32 NIV

Throughout her growing up years, Helen was physically abused by her father. The first chance she had to leave home, she took it. She didn't care if she never saw her father again.

When Helen met a co-worker who led her to Christ, her whole life changed. She received God's blessing of salvation and His provision of a spiritual family at church to help meet her needs.

She had grown substantially as a Christian, but there were still areas of her life that she struggled with. Helen realized that she was becoming more and more like the person she hated the most, her father. She knew that until she released her deep resentment toward him and blessed him, hatred would continue to have an iron grip on her life.

Helen finally made the most difficult decision in her life. She decided to visit her dad and ask his forgiveness for the anger and hatred she had carried toward him. As she poured out her heart, he asked her to forgive him for all the pain he had caused her. They were both in tears. Helen walked away free to live in the present because she was at last unchained from the past.

*Is unforgiveness keeping me chained to the past?*

*Beloved, let us love one another, for love is of God;
and everyone who loves is born of God and knows
God.*
                                        —1 JOHN 4:7

Yesterday we reflected on Helen's story: a woman who had the courage to ask forgiveness from a father who had physically abused her for years. How could someone so wounded find enough love in her heart to forgive one who had caused her so much pain?

Helen didn't have enough love on her own. But once she became a Christian, and was surrounded by a spiritual family that provided the warmth, love and acceptance she was missing, Helen was no longer alone.

It was God's love shown through the tangible concern of many people who cared about her that enabled Helen to feel blessed for the first time in her life. Becoming a member of a church that mutually cares for one another, prays for and encourages one another is one of the most important things you can do for yourself if you are working toward reclaiming the blessing in your life.

Helen could have been content to feel cared for by her friends at church. But their love did more than shelter and restore her: it also empowered her to become a source of blessing to others.

*God's Spirit and His people empower the impossible.*

> *See to it that no one misses the grace of God and*
> *that no bitter root grows up to cause trouble.*
> —HEB. 12:15 NIV

We are not responsible for our parents' actions, but we are responsible for our reactions to what they do. A sinful response like bitterness, for example, can spring up like a weed to choke out blessing. Only confession can release it.

Tom was angry at his father. Like so many driven fathers in our culture, Tom's dad had never been available for his son. Tom went to good colleges and was well provided for, but he resented his dad's absence.

To hurt him back, Tom moved across the country after college, got married, and didn't tell his dad for several years. When his father found out, he cried, something Tom had never seen him do. It wasn't until then that Tom realized how much his lies and deception had hurt his father.

Convicted of his sin, Tom confessed his bitterness in prayer and asked his father's forgiveness. As he did, he pictured Jesus loosening the root of bitterness lodged so long in his heart. In the empty hole that remained, Jesus planted a sprig of hyssop that gave off a fresh, minty aroma—the aroma of grace.

*Confession creates a clean heart.*

*For God has not given us a spirit of fear, but of power and of love and of a sound mind.*
—2 TIM. 1:7

It takes courage to change.

Perhaps you are aware that destructive patterns from the past are sabotaging your present and future happiness. Perhaps you recognize that something you do to your children (maybe a learned behavior from your past) lowers their self-worth and ties them in knots, and yet you put off changing. Why? Probably fear is preventing you from initiating that long-overdue change process.

You may be afraid that looking at the past, your parents' faults and your own mistakes, will be too painful. Perhaps you are afraid of the reaction you will get if you bring up past problems with loved ones. Or perhaps you fear that facing one problem in your life means you'll have to face others you are not ready for.

Fear can paralyze. However, if we choose to lay aside our timidity and boldly move out in God's love and power, God promises to dispel our fears.

Someone has said that the phrase "do not fear" appears in the Bible 365 times because God knows we need a reminder every day!

*Love flings open the door of possibility and empowers us to change.*

> *When Jesus saw him lying there, and knew that he already had been in that condition a long time, He said to him, "Do you want to be made well?"*
> —JOHN 5:6

The invalid by the pool of Bethesda had suffered from his condition for a long time. Thirty-eight years to be exact. Jesus asked him, "Do you want to get well?" This question was not meant to be cruel or mocking. It was meant to size up the man's motives.

People grow comfortable with the familiar, even if they are miserable in it. Women victims of domestic abuse frequently marry men who beat them as their father did. It is what they are used to. Self-pity can become a crutch and self-rationalization ("that's just the way I am") an excuse for slipping into complacency.

In our counseling, we see many people who want change, but are not willing to do anything to bring it about. Others don't follow through with change because they feel deep inside that hurtful patterns will go away on their own. Not dealing with problems is like having a broken watch and waiting for it to repair itself. It can keep you operating on the wrong time for years.

_____

*Do you want to get well?*

*And God will wipe away every tear from their
eyes . . . There shall be no more pain, for the
former things have passed away.*    **—REV. 21:4**

M an is born to trouble," as Job said. We tend to think
that our own trouble is far worse than anyone else's.

An ancient rabbinic parable offers an insightful perspective on suffering. The story is told that at judgment
everyone was called before the "suffering tree." All the
items of each person's suffering were laid out on a
branch of that tree. Every human being was allowed
to gaze upon the tree and pick which branch of suffering he would choose. An amazing thing happened. As
each person saw the suffering of all humanity laid out,
branch by branch, life by life, each one returned to his
own branch and decided to keep his own load of suffering.

Reclaiming the blessing is to a large degree growing
in God's compassion: seeing the suffering in each
heart, recognizing that those who hurt us are often
hurting too, and allowing our suffering to gift us to
reach out to others to dry a tear, help bear a burden,
hold out hope.

*As wounded healers, we can truly become a source of blessing for
others.*

*Those who are well have no need of a
physician . . . for I did not come to call the
righteous, but sinners, to repentance.*
                                    —MATT. 9:12–13

Another day, another deadline" read the cartoon
taped to Jeanette's computer. Jeanette looked blankly
at the cartoon, her computer's screen wondering if she
would ever finish her article. In the next room her
five-year-old daughter Susan implored, "Mom, will you
come play with us?" Jeanette had hardly seen her son
and daughter all day.

Jeanette thought that working at home would give
her more time with her children. But ever since she
left her full time job, her life had been filled with cleaning, writing, making dinner, writing, getting the kids
into bed, and more writing. This was not at all what
she had planned. Jeanette simply couldn't figure out
how to make it all work. As she looked back at her
computer screen she typed in the word, "failure."

Just as a tear of desperation formed in Jeanette's eye
she remembered the verse from her devotions that
morning, "Those who are well have no need of a physician." Jeanette thought *God, today I need a physician,
a housekeeper, a nanny, and six more hours in the day.
What I really need is you. Thank you for always being
here.*

---

*Lord, thank you for your salvation and your healing presence.*

*The people who walked in darkness have seen a
great light.*
—ISA. 9:2

Gretta knew what it was to walk in darkness. Born in Germany during the early days of World War II, she was the last of four children and unjustly blamed for all the family's problems. Notice of her father's death in the war arrived on Gretta's second birthday. Of course, it was her fault. As the family scapegoat, Gretta was hated by her mother and rejected by her siblings.

Gretta wanted desperately to see her life light up with warmth and acceptance, but when she plugged her life in to her natural family, the bulb remained dark or even worse, she received terrible shocks. Gretta tried plugging her life into anything that would give her power and life: friends, dating, school, jobs, drugs, and alcohol. She could never find the light she longed for.

Finally, Gretta discovered that she needed to plug into the Source of Life, Jesus Christ. In Him she felt unconditional love, for the first time. Her life lit up. With the decision to plug into God instead of others for her worth, Gretta began to release her past hurts.

*To whom or what do you look for your self-worth?*

*In Your light we see light.*
—PS. 36:9

With God lighting up her life and filling her with His love, Gretta began to see the truth about herself and those she loved.

Because she was no longer dependent on her mother to light up her life, Gretta was free to love her without expectations. She began to feel compassion for her mother instead of hate and to see her as a needy woman. At fifty-one, Gretta began calling her eighty-six-year-old mother and telling her that she loved her.

As they got to know one another, Gretta's mother shared hurts from her past. Gretta was amazed to discover that her mother had come from a home where there was almost constant sexual abuse. "No wonder she was never able to love me," Gretta told us in counseling.

With that admission, years of hurt and darkness in Gretta's life began to be replaced by a love for the Lord, for her family and even for herself that she had never before known. Instead of dishonoring her mother (and lowering her own worth as a result), Gretta made a decision to honor and value her—a decision that blessed them both.

———

*Lord, help me to see past my own hurt to recognize the hurt of others.*

*. . . God is light and in Him there is no darkness at all.*

—1 JOHN 1:5

Even though we are fully accepted and deeply loved by God, sometimes we don't *feel* loved and accepted. Something in us withholds trust. That something is often a distorted mental picture of who God is, based on hurtful childhood experiences and memories. For example, a child who grows up with harsh, demanding parents may have difficulty believing that God can really be affirming and loving.

The blessing many Christians need to reclaim is learning to see God as He really is—compassionate, gracious and full of steadfast love. God doesn't have a hidden dark streak. He really is a God of love, through and through.

To open ourselves fully to all the love that God longs to give, we often need to lay aside old baggage from our past, letting go of hurtful images that shape our view of what all parents are like.

In the coming days, as we reflect on different aspects of God, ask the Holy Spirit, the Spirit of truth, to heal any hurts that keep you from feeling close to your heavenly Father.

*Lord, help me to see You as You really are.*

> *God is our refuge and strength, a very present help in trouble.*
>
> —PS. 46:1

Even though the Bible tells us that God is ever-present, which should be a great comfort, many Christians feel that God is cold, distant, and unconcerned.

It was hard at first for Joyce to picture God as caring because her father, the son of restrained Scottish parents, never openly expressed affection and her mother was a complete stranger. Joyce never saw her mother. An alcoholic, her mother spent all day in bed upstairs. When Joyce went to a birthday party, her mother called a taxi to take her.

In college, Joyce accepted Christ and began to pray—tentatively. Her first answer to prayer was when her mother sought alcohol rehab treatment. Then He put godly people into Joyce's life—a husband who affirmed and valued her, friends who offered support in times of trouble.

"I've experienced God's presence in other people," said Joyce. She was, in turn, able to help her parents in their time of trouble. When her mother battled cancer and her father battled grief, God held them all in the palm of His hand.

*Lord, thank You for upholding me, even when I was not aware I was being carried by Another.*

*There is therefore now no condemnation to those
who are in Christ Jesus.*
—ROM. 8:1

To Sandy, God seemed mean and unforgiving. She knew this wasn't true and, as a Christian, felt guilty thinking that way. It's just that whenever she was naughty, people left her.

A childhood incident still haunted her. When she was ten, her sister had wanted to go to the movies one day. Sandy insisted they go swimming. It had been a cold day and Sandy's sister started shivering as soon as she got out of the water. The next day she came down with a virus that resulted in her death. Sandy always felt responsible because she had convinced her sister to go swimming and thought that had led to the virus. Soon after that, Sandy's parents divorced. Sandy also blamed herself for her dad's leaving.

Years later, Sandy's husband walked out. She thought of all the bad things she'd done to make him leave.

Sandy's healing came when God sent friends into her life who loved her despite her dark side. Through their total acceptance, she eventually came to see that God loved her unconditionally, too.

---

*Oh, Lord, thank You for loving me as I am. Help me to accept myself just as You do.*

*Draw near to God and He will draw near to you.*
—JAMES 4:8

It was hard for Brad to draw near to his heavenly Father because he felt such a great distance between himself and his earthly father. "He wasn't there," said Brad, recalling the pain of neglect. "He never had time for me."

Brad needed that emotional distance to be healed before he could feel close to God. In prayer, a friend helped Brad picture himself in the biblical scene of Jesus holding children in his lap and blessing them. Brad imagined himself as one of the children Jesus had held and blessed. Brad felt warm and secure, resting in Jesus' arms.

Then Brad's friend asked him to imagine his father as a little boy. Somehow, seeing his father equally as small and needy changed Brad's perspective of his dad. Loved and affirmed by Jesus, Brad became a different person. He became soft and relaxed, no longer angry. Brad invited his father up to sit in Jesus' lap, too.

Brad saw that Jesus had His arms around him *and* his dad so that they were one in His embrace. There, Brad found the healing he needed.

*Is Jesus calling you to be reconciled to a loved one to whom you feel distant?*

*Now the Lord is the Spirit, and where the Spirit of
the Lord is, there is freedom.* —2 COR. 3:17 NIV

Maureen's mother lived a circumscribed, safe life.
She was rigidly religious. As a daughter of an alcoholic
and the wife of an alcoholic, she survived the pain of
chaos by controlling as much of her environment as
possible.

Maureen, too, was a survivor. Years after leaving
home, she was happily married. The coping mecha-
nisms, however, that she had learned from her
mother—control and rigidity—made her life miserable. She met a Christian who was open and relaxed
about his faith. Maureen wanted that same inner
freedom.

Her friend told her that God loved her. He described
a God who wasn't anything like the harsh, punitive
God she had grown up with. As a child, Maureen had
learned not to trust and to expect disappointment after disappointment. It was hard to abandon herself to
a heavenly Father who loved her lavishly. But in time
she did, and found new joy.

*Father, help me live in Your spirit of freedom today.*

> *If you then, being evil, know how to give good gifts to your children, how much more will your Father who is in heaven give good things to those who ask Him!*
>
> —MATT 7:11

Marrera knew that God was a giver of good gifts. In fact, His gifts were so wonderful, they almost seemed too good to be true!

Whenever Marrera prayed and hoped for something and it became clear that God was going to give her the desire of her heart, she secretly feared that He would snatch it away at the last minute. Where did that deep distrust come from?

One day she understood. Her father, a product of the Depression, loved to lavish his children with gifts at Christmas. However, he didn't want the children to be spoiled or to take things for granted. Just before Christmas, Marrera would ask if she was going to receive the gifts she asked for. Her father would frown. "We'll see. There may not be enough money this year." Every year the gifts came, but every year his caution sowed anxiety in a little girl's heart.

Marrera smiled. Knowing where that anxiety came from released her from its power. She was able to open her arms wide and receive the good gifts God enjoyed giving.

*Heavenly Father, thank You for Your good gifts.*

*You have saved the best till now.*
—JOHN 2:10 NIV

While researching our book *The Blessing*, we asked a Bible study group to evaluate the material. Commenting on what her husband had learned, one wife wrote: "Dennis has learned so much about how to bless the children. It has made a real difference in his relationship with them. How about teaching him to bless me!!!"

Husbands and wives need to know they're loved and accepted as much as the children. The elements of the blessing that we've shared are not just limited to parent/child relationships. They can also be used to transform marriages.

The Gospels tell us that the purpose of Jesus' first miracle was to bring joy. At a wedding feast in Cana the wine ran out. To save the host embarrassment, Jesus changed six jars of plain water into the tastiest wine the guests had ever sampled.

You may feel that your marriage has lost its flavor, its sparkle. Even now, God's blessing can transform it from an ordinary relationship into something special, just as He did the wine that day at Cana.

---

*Yes, Lord, renew my marriage.*

*The two shall become one flesh.*
—EPH. 5:31

This well-known phrase is often read at weddings to paint a picture of how intimately interwoven man and woman will be as husband and wife. They enter into marriage as separate individuals, but over the years become one.

The first man and woman were literally one. God created Adam out of dust, but Eve was fashioned out of Adam's rib—"bone of my bones and flesh of my flesh" (Gen. 2:23). This physical interrelatedness suggests how deeply connected God intended husband and wife to be.

In the light of this, the first element of the blessing, meaningful touch, has great importance in blessing both partners in a marriage. A child needs to be held by a parent to have a sense of belonging. Just so a husband and wife use physical affection to say: "You belong to me. You are special. I feel one with you."

When two people are first attracted to one another, physical affection plays a big part in their relationship. Romance may cool, but the hunger to be touched never disappears.

*Say it with a touch, "I love you!"*

*And they were both naked, the man and his wife,
and were not ashamed.* —GEN. 2:25

God created man and woman and blessed their sexuality. In God's original plan, husband and wife felt so secure in His love and their own, they completely accepted themselves and each other. Their masculinity and femininity were great gifts, a beautiful blend of differences and celebration of coming together.

We often look at lovers with envy. They are so enthralled with one another they may kiss in public, comfortably wrap their arms around each other, stroll hand in hand, and laugh. Love can, indeed, be a many splendored thing—fresh, new, exciting.

How can we keep that sexual excitement in marriage? Vicki noticed that after her husband came home from a business trip, she felt a greater physical attraction for him. It was as if she were being reintroduced to him. They strolled around the block hand in hand and booked a hotel room to enjoy one another in a new setting.

Looking at our partners with new eyes can excite the desire to touch again and come close.

*I will see my husband with new eyes today.*

*Eat, O friends, and drink;*
*drink your fill, O lovers.*
—SONG 5:1 NIV

In our culture, which emphasizes sexuality, husbands and wives almost feel cheated when the original aura of physical attraction wears off. We're meant always to be lovers! God created sex for pleasure as well as having children.

In later years, when love matures, touch can be even more meaningful. Becoming more attuned to each other's bodies makes touch in the bedroom more enjoyable. Sexual touch provides physical relaxation and it is one way that adults play and have fun together.

Sadly, though, with so many husbands and wives both working now, many couples return home too fatigued to enjoy each other.

Fatigue, though, is not the only reason husbands and wives withhold physical touch. Emotional blocks, such as resentment and unforgiveness, also stop couples from touching.

Sex is a good gift. God created it and blessed it. Shouldn't we?

*Lord, help me to "stay in touch" with my husband.*

*Again, if two lie down together, they will keep*
*warm; but how can one be warm alone?*
—ECCL. 4:11

Touch not only blesses our relationship physically, giving us pleasure, but it also strengthens the emotional bond that is so vital to intimacy. At the end of the day, it is good to be restored in the arms of someone we love.

A woman in ministry, who had helped a number of friends through grief and divorce, felt crushed under the burdens she helped carry. Writing in her journal, she described the solace of being comforted by a loving husband: "As wave after wave of pain rolls over me, it wears me down. I feel vulnerable, weakened. I need another to lend me strength. Lying last night in the circle of Matt's arms, I felt protected, safe. I was able to rest and sink into a deep sleep."

Even though studies show that women, more than men, express a greater emotional need to be held, men also need the refuge of a warm embrace when they feel stressed or burdened.

—

*What a wonderful resource our arms are to comfort and soothe!*

> *Do not harden your hearts.*
> —PS. 95:8

Even small acts of touch—walking through a park hand in hand, snuggling close on a sofa in front of a crackling fire—nourish a marriage. Without that emotional nourishment, hearts can grow hard.

Listen to the sadness expressed in this word picture of a neglected wife: "When I was first married, I felt like a beautiful, handcrafted, leather-bound, gold-trimmed book that had been presented to my husband as a gift from God. At first I was received with great enthusiasm and excitement—cherished, talked about, shared with others, and handled with care. As time has gone by, I've been put on the bookshelf to collect dust. Once in awhile he remembers I'm here. But if only he would take me off the shelf and open me up! If only he'd see how much more I have to offer him!"

You can sense from these words that this husband and wife feel very distant from one another. Early on in their marriage, this adoring husband handled his wife with tender loving care. Now he doesn't "handle" or touch her at all!

How vital touch is to communicating closeness and caring.

*Lord, keep my heart soft and responsive today.*

*A word fitly spoken is like apples of gold in settings of silver.*
—PROV. 25:11

God has given us a rich repertoire of ways to affirm and value our husbands. Becoming fluent in the non-spoken language of touch is a wonderful way to strengthen our marriages. That powerful tool, available to us all, lies at the end of our fingertips. Another equally effective blessing tool lies on the tip of our tongues: spoken words of praise.

Parents may be conscientious in blessing their children with praise to build up their self-esteem, but forget completely that everyone needs to hear words of praise and encouragement.

In counseling couples, we often ask wives and husbands to praise at least one thing they appreciate about their spouse each day for thirty days—one month. Just doing this often causes positive changes in relationships.

Try it. Just a few words like "Honey, you are so good with the kids," or "You're as handsome, today, as you are wonderful," can enrich almost any marriage. Remember to affirm your husband's character (patient, generous, thoughtful) not just what he does. Don't let your husband know you are doing this.

*Have your praised your husband today?*

*A kind word cheers him up.*
—PROV. 12:25 NIV

Creative presentation adds to the fun and flair of sharing words of blessing. A few years ago, I (John) had to fly out of town on a publicity tour over Valentine's Day. Before I left, I took Cindy out to dinner, gave her a card and flowers. However, over those expressions of love for my wife stood one small gift.

I gave Cindy a clothespin, just a standard, wooden, five-cent clothespin, with the heart-felt words, "Honey, you do such a great job of holding the whole family together with all our busy schedules—I wanted you to have this clothespin."

The first thing I saw when I got home was that clothespin in a prominent place on our refrigerator door. Cindy had glued a magnet to the back of it and drawn a red heart in front. It was now a permanent reminder of those few words of blessing I'd shared.

Another weary husband, coming home from a business trip, found a fortune cookie on his pillow. With it was a note from his wife, "How fortune-ate I am to have you for a husband. Welcome home!"

*Lord, remind me daily to drop seeds of affirmation into the soil of my husband's heart.*

*How beautiful you are, my darling! Oh, how
beautiful!*
                                        —SONG 1:15 NIV

Solomon, the wisest man in the world, was an arduous bridegroom extravagantly praising his new bride with glowing compliments. Solomon's example provides a godly picture of what courtship and marriage should be. When we greatly value our marriage partner, God is delighted.

Solomon's repeated words of affirmation did wonders for the shy, insecure young woman who was to become his wife. When she first met this dashing young king, the Shulamite woman was ashamed of her appearance. "Do not look upon me, because I am dark" (Song 1:6). Solomon specifically affirms what she devalues in herself, "O fairest among women . . . your cheeks are lovely" (vv 8, 10). Seeing herself as lovely in Solomon's eyes, she begins to affirm herself, "I am the rose of Sharon, and the lily of the valleys" (2:1). In essence, she is saying, "Yes, I *am* beautiful."

Our self-talk (the words we tell ourselves about who we are) is often overally critical. Words of affirmation from someone we love can make a dramatic difference in how we see ourselves.

*Lord, help me to show my husband my delight in him by using affirming words.*

> *He has endowed you with splendor.*
> —ISA. 55:5 NIV

Debra knew she should never have been born. Her mother told her, repeatedly, that she wished she had aborted her. Debra's father said he wished she had been a boy. Debra grew up feeling worthless and unwanted.

One day, Debra met a man who saw her differently. He saw a beautiful treasure hidden within a sullen college girl dressed in jeans and flannel shirts. Bill began to praise Debra with gentle, tender words of affirmation, words that were sorely lacking in her life. Adored for the first time by a man, Debra began to discover her femininity. Her clothes became softer, her eyes bright.

Just as Solomon had sung praises to his shy bride, Bill would spontaneously break out in song when he was dating Debra, expressing how much he loved her and how much God loved her.

"You were meant to be born, meant to be a woman," he assured her. "You came out just the way God wanted you to be. You're worth a lot to me."

Bill's words were like sunshine to a tiny spring bud waiting to blossom. Gradually, his warmth brought forth the full flower of Debra's inner beauty.

---

*I will sing my husband's praises today.*

*As the bridegroom rejoices over the bride, so shall
your God rejoice over you.*                    —ISA. 62:5

Your husband may not be a man of many words. He
may be the strong, silent type who doesn't say anything at all!

This was Barbara's problem. When she and Kirk
first fell in love, he felt free to verbally express his love
to Barbara. But as the years went by, Kirk settled into
silence, like his father, a man who could not openly
share his feelings.

Barbara felt starved for words of affection. As she
was reading the Bible one day, she came across this
passage about God rejoicing over His loved ones like
a bridegroom. A picture popped into her mind of a
wedding ceremony. She saw herself as a bride walking
down the aisle. Jesus stood at the end of the aisle waiting for her. His eyes lit up in adoration as a groom be-
holds his bride.

Barbara felt deeply loved at that moment. That picture came back many times in prayer and was a great
comfort. Whenever she came across Christ's loving
words in Scripture, she drank them in as an expression
of His affection for her. One day, Kirk would be able
to say those words. Until then, she felt cherished by
another Bridegroom.

*Lord of love, thank You for lavishing me with affection. I feel loved.*

> *And how is it that we hear, each in our own*
> *language in which we were born?* —ACTS 2:8

There are many ways to say, "I love you." Barbara didn't feel her husband loved her because he didn't express his affection in words. However, there were times when he shouted the message loud and clear in ways that *he* understood.

Kirk enjoyed bringing gifts home to Barbara after business trips. Rather than receiving them with joy, Barbara felt resentful at Kirk's absence and saw his presents as a means to appease his conscience for being away. Barbara completely missed the message.

When Barbara would verbally express her love for Kirk, he missed the message too. He felt her words were empty, unless she showed him how much she cared through specific actions.

The way Barbara and Kirk communicated affection derived from "the language in which they were born"—from their families-of-origin.

They had to learn to speak one another's language. This took attentive listening, clarifying, and a willingness to broaden their communication base.

*Teach me to speak my husband's love language, Lord.*

*By my God I can leap over a wall.*
—2 SAM. 22:30

Sometimes words meant to bless meet a wall of resistance. An insecure spouse may hear a compliment, but not really accept it. One way to get around these defenses is to use a word picture that sends a message to the heart, not the head.

Alan lost his first wife to cancer; nine years later he married a cute, petite blonde named Charlotte. Charlotte loved Alan dearly, but Alan had a deep-seated fear that his pretty wife would leave him for a younger man.

Charlotte wanted to let her husband know how much he really meant to her. In front of friends and family at a birthday party, she told them all a story. She described herself as a cocker spaniel who grew up in a home that didn't accept such lively dogs. She was told she was a mongrel who wasn't worth anything. One day Alan gently picked her up, washed and brushed her dirty, matted coat, and treated her like a purebred champion. "Honey," she said, "you are the greatest gift in my life."

Alan was so deeply touched by his wife's tribute that six years of insecurity and unfounded fear were swept away. He never doubted her love again.

*Lord, help me to let my husband know that he is secure in my love.*

> *Now faith is the subtance of things hoped for, the*
> *evidence of things not seen.*
> —HEB. 11:1

Word pictures can not only be used to praise a husband or wife, they can also be used to discuss sensitive issues that are difficult to bring up. By using a word picture instead of lashing out with damaging words, we can often get across a message we can't seem to get across any other way.

Teresa sensed that her marriage was in trouble and felt that counseling would help. She had tried to convince Tom to go, but he didn't see the need.

One day when they sat on the back porch, she turned to Tom. "You see that ivy, Tom?" "It's dying." Forgotten on the back porch, the once gorgeous plant looked pathetic. Without water, it was bone dry. The leaves were withered and brown, dropping off. "That's what I feel our marriage is like now because we've neglected it. It could be so much more!"

Tom finally understood. The next day, when Teresa glanced at the back porch, she couldn't believe her eyes. There hung a huge ivy, green and flourishing in place of the old one. It was Tom's way of saying, "Yes, you're right. I value our marriage too. Let's create something new."

*Lord, thank You that Your mercies are new every morning, and so are marriages.*

*One star differs from another star in glory.*
—1 COR. 15:41

One way to attach high value to a spouse is to appreciate each other's uniqueness.

Bill was a rugged outdoorsman who moved his family outside the city so he could be closer to hunting and fishing. Betty was a petite city girl who loved to socialize. At first, Betty enjoyed backpacking with her husband, but when their two children came along, Bill went camping on his own. Isolated from her friends, Betty grew resentful.

When Bill and Betty came to see me (Gary) for counseling, they were angry and defensive. Each accused the other of being insensitive.

To help them view each other in a new way, I imagined them both as pictures hanging on a wall. In Bill's picture, I could see him standing proudly near a mountain stream, with a doe and newborn fawns in the background. In Betty's, I saw her as a delicate, beautiful wildflower with dazzling colors. I challenged them to look at the beauty in the other person's picture for a week.

They came back a changed couple. Instead of dishonoring one another with anger, they became more patient by valuing each other's differences.

*Together my husband and I will complete each other.*

> *One thing I know: that though I was blind, now I see.*
> **—JOHN 9:25**

It is so easy in marriage to see things from only one point of view. Stubbornly we're entrenched in our own self-interest. The whole world seems to revolve around personal needs, personal desires, personal hurts.

Julia lay awake in the darkness thinking about her husband who was out-of-town that night. He seemed so distant from her. He poured himself into his work, played racquetball at the sports club after work, and retreated behind the newspaper when he came home. Was he even aware of her existence?

Julia had a sudden inspiration to roll over on his side of the bed. She imagined herself as Steve looking across at her at night. How did he perceive her?

She accused him of not being there for her, but was she there for him? She poured herself into activities that interested her, became absorbed in projects, talked on the phone to friends.

What an eye-opener! How self-centered she was! Julia decided to confess her neglect to Steve and ask for his forgiveness.

---

*Open my eyes, Lord, to my own insensitivity before I accuse others of hurting me.*

*He who has ears to hear, let him hear!*
—MATT. 11:15

Expressing high value to our marriage partners means not only seeing things from their point of view but also listening attentively to their needs. Most marriage guides suggest setting aside an evening for couples to be together alone and to concentrate on their relationship. Dinner dates are important, but it's just as important to build listening times into our daily schedules.

"We have our best conversations at noon," says Pam, whose husband calls her every day during his lunch break. They developed the habit when they were both working in the early years of their marriage. Now that Pam stays home, she values their noon-time chats even more. "It's a time to connect during the day, a very focused time—no TV, no distractions, the boys are at school." If Mark has to go out to lunch with clients, he still calls Pam just to check in.

Taking time in our busy schedules to listen to each other keeps the lines of communication open and shows we respect and care about the person we married.

*Lord, teach me to listen, really listen, to my husband.*

> *Now may the God of patience and comfort grant*
> *you to be like-minded toward one another.*
> —ROM. 15:5

Being open and responsive in daily communication helps us keep our fingers on the pulse of what's going on inside our spouse. It is also the best preventive measure to keep everyday irritations from becoming life-threatening to a healthy marriage.

One day Mark came home from work ebullient. He and Pam had just bought a new house and he loved it. "I hated going to work today and missing all the fun here," he said as they chatted while Pam made dinner.

Mark's effusiveness irritated Pam. "No fun happened here today, Mark. I haven't had *any* fun." She told him that in the middle of the day, overwhelmed by piles of boxes, a kitchen half re-modeled, things strewn everywhere, she sat down and cried, horribly depressed.

Mark was shocked and silent. He'd had no idea what Pam was going through.

Because the lines of communication were open in their marriage, Mark and Pam were able to talk through Pam's frustrations. A conflict, which could have been divisive, brought them closer.

_____

*Give me Your ears and eyes, Lord, to help me tune in to my husband's needs.*

*Do not let the sun go down while you are still*
*angry, and do not give the devil a foothold.*
—EPH. 4:26–27 NIV

Anything can become divisive in a marriage: children, finances, career plans, values, priorities, habits. The list is endless. If two people do not value each other's needs, it is easy for marriage to become a tug-of-war between two angry opponents.

Anger is such a serious problem in all relationships that the Bible warns us to resolve angry disputes right away. If we nurse our anger, there are serious consequences. We've talked to many couples in counseling who attend church and love God, but still have not found peace. One of the major reasons for their failure is deep-seated anger. Unwilling to forgive or seek forgiveness, they harbor secret darkness in their lives that, like termites to wood, eats away at the foundation of their happy home.

Kathy and Dan are aware of this danger. As a constant reminder, they have a plaque over their bed that reads, "Do Not Let the Sun Go Down on Your Anger." They are committed to resolving their differences daily.

---

*I will keep short accounts.*

*Can two walk together, unless they are agreed?*
—AMOS 3:3

Marriage begins with a solemn stroll down a church aisle together. Newlyweds continue to stroll hand in hand down the same path for some time, excited to be in each other's company, sharing the same hopes and dreams, a common vision.

But as healthy individuals who allow each other the freedom to grow, husband and wife begin to walk divergent paths, which is fine as long as they come together again. We are complex people with ever-changing needs. Circumstances, other people, self-reflection all work together to change us, day by day. How common is the cry of a married partner, "You are not the same person I married." Of course not!

There are times in any healthy marriage when spouses need to renegotiate their agreement. It is easy to sweep conflicts under the rug: "I thought that might be bothering him, but he didn't say anything so I let it go."

As we work out our differences, we are not only standing on common ground, but holy ground, where God can birth new hopes, new dreams, and perhaps reveal a new path not yet explored.

*Openly airing your feelings can open the door to new possibilities.*

*Therefore a man shall leave his father and mother
and be joined to his wife, and they shall become
one flesh.*

—GEN. 2:24

Kim wanted a family wedding. She had grown up in
a close-knit family that did everything together. Karl
had always assumed they'd elope as his parents did.
Why make a big fuss? Kim and Karl had known each
other for four years before they started discussing
wedding plans. They were astonished how much their
expectations differed! Twenty years later they are still
grappling with the differences between their families-
of-origin.

This is not unusual. Leaving our parents to become
one with someone else is not as easy as packing a suit-
case and moving across town. The inner baggage we
carry with us may take years to unpack and sort out.

Seeing things from our limited point of view, we
tend to defend our way of doing things as superior, or
worse yet think of it as the only way. One of the most
significant ways we can attach high value to our
spouse is to respect his background.

Then, with gentleness and understanding, we can
weave together a new oneness out of the best of both
families.

*Lord, give me patience as we sort out the past and put together a
new future.*

*Your ears shall hear a word behind you, saying,*
*"This is the way, walk in it."* —ISA. 30:21

At times, even the best marriages can get off track. God has given husbands and wives special tools with which to communicate—meaningful touch, words to express emotions and thoughts, ways to know one another deeply. However, we sometimes forget to use these tools or we abuse them. Intimacy can be so easily lost.

"So that was it," said one husband as his wife confessed to having an affair. "I felt like I was groping around in the dark. I didn't know what was wrong."

Is there any way back when married partners stray out of each other's arms? When their communication is in shambles and they stand alone in darkness?

Yes. That is, when our ears are open to the One who knows the path—even in the darkness. When we have run out of words of love, He can give us a new vocabulary; when our hands are too weary to reach across a chasm of misunderstanding, He stands in the gap, His hands outstretched to heal.

God has given us tools to communicate. He has also given us tools to restore intimacy: confession, forgiveness, reconciliation. They are part of the blessing, too.

*Jesus, thank You for standing in the gap, always drawing my husband and me closer to one another and to You.*

*Then He who sat on the throne said, "Behold, I make all things new."*
—REV. 21:5

Eric walked out on Darlene at 4:05 P.M. She knew because she stopped the clock on the living room wall then, and would not restart it until he came back. Their marriage, like that clock, remained frozen in time.

She wasn't surprised that Eric walked out. There had been physical abuse, emotional abuse. Lots of screaming. Lots of anger. Lots of shame. He wanted a divorce, but she didn't.

Darlene knew there were problems, big problems, but she still loved Eric deeply and wanted to make their marriage work. To resolve their conflicts she knew they needed help.

Eric agreed to go to a Christian counselor. In a safe, caring environment, they were both free to air their grievances. They learned constructive ways to dialogue and respect each other. They were held accountable for their actions week by week. Gradually, their marriage began to move forward again and so did the clock.

---

*God can make all things new, even things that feel fixed forever.*

*Bear with each other and forgive whatever*
*grievances you may have against one another.*
*Forgive as the Lord forgave you.* —COL. 3:13 NIV

Eric and Darlene were able to improve their marriage because they put into practice the fourth element of the blessing, picturing a special future. This meant letting go of a fixed assumption—"things will never change"—and giving each other a second chance.

For many people, it is harder to picture a special future for a spouse than it is for the children. We tend to make allowances for children: they're learning; they make mistakes; tomorrow is a new day. We are less forgiving with someone we've been married to for twenty years: he *always* does that; he'll *never* change. And how can a wife be understanding when she is the victim of a husband's destructive habits?

It is helpful to remember that Christ died for us while we were still sinners (see Rom. 5:8). He didn't wait for us to change and be worthy of His love. It is because of His love, freely given, that we can change.

We are asked to believe the best in each other just as Jesus believes the best in us.

*"Always" and "never" are not words found in the vocabulary of reconciliation.*

*Above all things have fervent love for one another,
for "love will cover a multitude of sins."*
—1 PETER 4:8

*Give my husband a second chance? No way!* thought Laura, *not after the way he'd hurt me.* Laura's husband was a truck driver, often out of town. When he was home, he drank and made her life miserable.

Laura was ready to file for a divorce when a close friend recommended she see her pastor first. She went reluctantly. After listening to Laura's description of her husband's faults, the pastor was silent for a few minutes. Then he said, "Have you ever forgiven your husband for all his many faults?"

Laura was stunned. What a crazy idea! But later she began to think about what he said. A week later in the pastor's study, she surrendered her life to Christ and decided to forgive her husband and love him unconditionally.

As Laura's life was changed by the Source of Blessing Himself, she began to bless her husband by building him up and encouraging him. Her husband was so amazed by his wife's changed behavior that he also decided to go to the pastor to ask for help with his drinking problem.

*It is never too late to begin again.*

*The Lord gives freedom to the prisoners.*
—PS. 146:7

Picturing a special future for our spouse means giving them room to grow.

Beth loved Mike, but after fifteen years of marriage, she sensed that the freedom and acceptance they had enjoyed when they were first married was being replaced by an oppressive critical spirit, a lack of elasticity. There was no longer any "give" in their relationship.

She blamed Mike for his rigidity until one day God showed her a picture in prayer. She saw Mike as a butterfly with her hands cupped over him. "Let him go," God seemed to say. "Surrender him to Me."

How could she let him go? First, she realized that her expectations were limiting Mike, not allowing him the freedom to be himself. Secondly, she needed to appreciate who he was, focusing on the things he did well, instead of complaining about his shortcomings.

Beth felt convicted to change. It was hard. She would let go, then tighten the reigns of control again; she would praise, then complain. But gradually a new openness came to their marriage, a new grace.

*Lord, help me to surrender the reigns of control in my marriage.*

*Confess your trespasses [sins] to one another, and
pray for one another, that you may be healed.*
—JAMES 5:16

Have you ever struggled under the weight of grocery
bags too heavy to carry and had some kind soul gently
ask, "Can I help you?" You sigh with relief and gratitude as the burden is lifted out of your hands. You feel
light as a feather.

That is how wonderful it feels to let go of the burden
of unconfessed sin. Control is a sin. To take full responsibility for someone else's life, to try to manipulate
their behavior and make things come out the way we
want them to is very tempting for caregivers, but a sin.
Most women succumb to this temptation in marriage.

You can let go of this burden through prayer, confessing it to a trusted friend or counselor. Putting your
hands palm down on the uplifted hands of another
helps you picture relinquishing it into the gentle hands
of Jesus.

Struggling with a troubled marriage, Silvia did this.
"I've felt so alone in this for so long," she wrote in her
journal. "I sense such peace now in releasing my need
to fix things and acknowledge that God is in control."

*Lord, help me to let go, to confess rather than cover up my part in
a conflict.*

> *And Jesus said to her, "Neither do I condemn you;*
> *go and sin no more."*
> —JOHN 8:11

Sometimes picturing a special future involves forgiving ourselves, not a spouse.

Ruth sat in a Sunday school class where the seventh commandment was being discussed, "Thou shalt not commit adultery." She wondered what Ralph was thinking.

Ten years ago she had been involved in an extramarital affair. Even though Ralph had forgiven her, she could not forgive herself. Ruth said nothing during the discussion, but Ralph spoke up: "It's never one person's fault. Even the wronged partner is partly responsible." Ruth was amazed to hear him say that. It was as if he were defending and supporting her.

What would people in that class think if they knew? She pictured herself as the woman in the story. She felt petrified, imagining her classmates stoning her with their stares. She felt ugly, ashamed. Suddenly she was aware of a warm presence in the room. She looked up and saw Jesus. There was no condemnation in His eyes, only love. She felt a deep peace.

Finally, in that moment of mercy, she felt fully forgiven. Two wonderful men had set her free.

---

*I will show mercy to those I love.*

*What God has joined together, let not man
separate.*                                    —MARK 10:9

The fifth element of the blessing is active commitment. Just as blessing our children is a lifelong pursuit, so it takes incredible tenacity to make a lasting commitment in marriage.

In our culture, we marry for love and hope that both partners will eventually become lifelong partners and friends. In many West African countries, the order is reversed. Families arrange marriages, bringing together two young people as a friendly alliance, and hope that they will eventually fall in love. "After thirty years," said an African father to his son, "I am now in love with your mother."

God's plan for marriage is a lifetime commitment: a man and woman maturing together, growing together, supporting each other as individuals and as one. Impossible? No, not really. Difficult? Undoubtedly.

Marriage is a marathon, not a quick sprint. The obstacles are many; the odds against commitment, daunting. But it is important to remember that God is more committed to making our marriage work than we are.

*Lord, give me the staying power to keep on keeping on.*

> *Now may the God of hope fill you with all joy and*
> *peace in believing, that you may abound in hope*
> *by the power of the Holy Spirit.*   —ROM. 15:13

Judy felt weak, as if all the breath had been knocked out of her. Another angry argument had dealt a deadly blow to their marriage. Sitting beside her husband on the plane, she felt deeply depressed. Doug was cold and far away. She sensed that he wanted out of their marriage.

In despair, Judy cried out to God. In prayer, she saw the heart of their marriage as a literal heart. It lay on the floor, ripped out, bruised and bleeding. Its beat was very slow and labored. There seemed to be so little life left.

Then Judy saw Jesus tenderly pick up the failing heart in His hands. Only His hands could make it strong. Only His hands had the power. Suddenly the heart was transformed, exploding into a starburst of light. Judy recognized that radiance as God's glory and knew, in a penetrating way, that Jesus was going to love their marriage back to life. Not just to restore it, but make it far better than she could ever imagine.

Judy's depression lifted. That vision of hope, given as a gift, in prayer, renewed her hope for her marriage. Just as God promised, it did improve.

*Lord, bless my marriage with hope today.*

*Two are better than one, . . . for if they fall, one will lift up his companion. But woe to him who is alone when he falls, for he has no one to help him up.*

—ECCL. 4:9–10

All marathon runners dread "hitting the wall," that point in the race when weariness and fatigue overtake you; that point when you think you just can't take one more faltering step.

I (John) remember feeling that way one time. I had finished my B.A. and Th.M. and was dashing ahead to enter a doctoral program. I had applied to an out-of-state university and was sure I'd get in. I told all my friends about it; my fiancé and I planned and dreamed about it for months.

Then came the rejection letters. I was devastated. Why had I told so many people about this? What would Cindy think?

When Cindy found out about the rejection, she fixed me a great dinner. She listened as I poured out my hurt and disappointment.

Cindy assured me that God could still use me, that I was already "Dr. Trent" in her eyes. Her faith in me gave me a renewed strength to get up and keep going. A few weeks later I received a letter of acceptance from an outstanding doctoral program.

All through our marriage Cindy has supported and encouraged me, cheering me on, rain or shine.

---

*I will be my husband's best fan.*

> *Bear one another's burdens, and so fulfill the law*
> *of Christ.*
> —GAL. 6:2

Marriages require give and take. Sometimes it may seem as if one partner does all the giving, but over the years the tables keep turning and turning.

After surviving the ups and downs of forty-five years of marriage, Elaine had thought the retirement years would be easy sailing. But retirement, like all stages of marriage, has its own stresses. She was surprised at how irritable and demanding a husband, suddenly stripped of responsibility, could be. However, remembering her earlier years helped put the present into perspective.

"When we were younger," said Elaine, "Norm was very patient with me, even though I deserved a swift kick. I would be short-tempered and he would grab my hand and say, 'Calm down. I'm your best friend.' Now I need to be the understanding one."

Active commitment means mutual burden-bearing: forgiving because you've been forgiven, putting out your hand to support someone because you were once the one who needed support, and making sacrifices because someone once sacrificed for you.

---

*Lord, help me to focus on the long-term view of my marriage instead of short-term irritations.*

*His love endures forever.*
—PS. 136:1 NIV

Ron was Penny's first close friend. Penny had yearned for an intimate relationship, but she always kept people at arm's length. If they came too close, she was afraid they might not like what they saw.

But Ron was different. He came close, saw everything there was to see, and accepted Penny as she was, flaws and all. He was the first person in Penny's life to offer her unconditional love. First as a friend, then as a husband, Ron began to bless Penny.

"He touched me and spoke words of love to me, telling me how valuable I was to him. I knew we had a special future, because he also made an active commitment."

Of all the elements of the blessing, Penny said his commitment meant the most. Penny's parents were never there for her so she frequently tested Ron to see if his love was real. Acting out anger from the past, she might scream or throw a chair or cruelly bait Ron in a war of words. Calmly, he would help Penny get to the source of her pain and anger, and resolve it.

"I'm never going away," Ron promised. And he hasn't. Like the Father, he is there forever.

*Thank You, Lord, for Your lasting commitment to me and my marriage.*

> *It may be that the LORD will look on my*
> *affliction, and . . . repay me with good for*
> *[t]his cursing this day.*
> —2 SAM. 16:12

The active commitment David's wife showed to her husband brought about a miracle.

David lay in a hospital bed, no longer a handsome man. He had been severely wounded in Vietnam by a grenade that exploded near his ear. The soldier who lay next to him was also grotesquely disfigured. That man's wife arrived from the States, took one look at her husband and took off her wedding ring. "I'm so sorry," she said, "but there's no way I could live with you looking like that."

After observing this, David dreaded his own wife's arrival. But she, a strong Christian, had a very different response. She kissed him on the only place where his face wasn't bandaged and said, "Honey, I love you. I'll always love you. I want you to know that whatever it takes, whatever the odds, we can make it, together."

Knowing what had happened to the other soldier and then experiencing his wife's love for him gave David tremendous strength. Miraculously, he recovered. Years later on national TV, he was able to say, "I am twice the person I was before I went to Vietnam. The Lord has let me have a worldwide, positive effect on people's lives because of what I went through."

*Thank You that whatever comes, Lord, we can make it together.*

*But there is a friend who sticks closer than a brother.*

—PROV. 18:24

Cultivating the elements of the blessing in our homes can bring a rich harvest of love and joy. However, as we said earlier, these principles can also be applied to enrich our other relationships as well. Let's look at how the blessing can strengthen friendships.

Everyone needs friends—close friends—for encouragement, for support, for understanding, and so much more.

When we walk into a crowd our eyes scan the room searching for something. The hors d'oeuvre table? The entertainment? No. More than likely, we are on the lookout for a face we recognize, a friend we feel close to.

When we find that friend, how do we feel? Comfortable. Secure. We can chat to scores of acquaintances, but what our heart seeks like a homing device is that one good friend. Someone who knows us, shares our interests and concerns, and speaks the same language.

Oh, the joy of being understood, being appreciated, being valued by a friend!

*Thank You, Lord, for my friends and how much they mean to me. Teach me to bless them, as You would.*

> *The soul of Jonathan was knit to the soul of David,*
> *and Jonathan loved him as his own soul.*
> —1 SAM. 18:1

Jonathan and David were soul-mates, the closest kind of friends. In Scripture, their friendship is held up as a model of an intimate, lasting relationship. How did they become so close, their souls so deeply inter-woven?

It didn't just happen. Like all meaningful relation-ships, the fabric of their friendship was stitched to-gether with intentional words and actions of affection. Their friendship included every aspect of giving the blessing: meaningful touch, spoken words of affection, expressing high value, picturing a special future, and active commitment. There is much that we can learn from their example.

"To have a friend," it has been said, "you have to be a friend." Perhaps you have trouble making friends or keeping friends or getting closer to the friends you do have. Because we are made in God's image, made for relationships, it is natural that we should long to grow closer to our friends or feel a sadness if we don't have close friends.

Ask God to show you how to become a Jonathan or David in your friendships.

------

*Jesus, what a friend You are to me! Help me to be that kind of friend to others.*

*And Jonathan took off the robe that was on him and gave it to David, with his armor, even to his sword and his bow and his belt.*   —1 SAM. 18:4

Who can say what drew Jonathan to David? Their's was an unlikely friendship. Jonathan, the son of the king of Israel, was a mighty warrior. He met David just after the shepherd boy had slain Goliath and had become Israel's hero. Jonathan could have been jealous of David and feared him as a rival, but he didn't. Instead, the two young men became great friends.

Jonathan valued David highly. He not only praised his friend verbally, but he also showed his appreciation for David by a significant gesture. In ancient Israel, a warrior only laid down his weapons in front of someone he considered better than himself. When Jonathan gave David his armor and robes, symbols of his authority, he was demonstrating how much he honored his friend.

Remember the word *bless* literally means "to bow the knee." To show reverence and honor to an important person.

"I admire you. I treasure your special qualities," are loving messages sent by word and action that bless a friendship.

*Today I will honor a friend.*

> *And they kissed one another; and they wept*
> *together, but David more so.*   —1 SAM. 20:41

Unfortunately, Jonathan's father, King Saul, did not share his son's affection for David. As David's prestige grew, Saul became jealous and plotted to kill David. The verse we're reflecting on today describes the tremendous emotion Jonathan and David felt when they realized it was no longer safe for them to be together.

This final expression of closeness shows that these two men were not afraid to express their emotions openly and to demonstrate their affection through meaningful touch. It was probably indicative of the way they had blessed their relationship all along the way with close physical contact.

In our culture, seeing two men put their arms around one another may produce immediate, negative assumptions, but this is not unusual in other cultures.

A warm hug, a touch on the arm, a hand on a shoulder all draw friends closer—men as well as women.

---

*Reach out and touch your friend.*

*The LORD be with you as He has been with my father.*
                                    —1 SAM. 20:13

Before Jonathan and David parted, they vowed their commitment toward one another through a spoken covenant. As they felt comfortable enough to express their affection through touch, they also showed how much they valued each other by words of affirmation.

Certainly one secret to a flourishing friendship is the verbal expression of affirmation. "Thank you for being more special to me than all the wrapable gifts there are," wrote one friend. Another woman thanked her friend for bringing so much joy into her life with these words she wrote in a greeting card, "You gather up the colors of my life and weave them into rainbows for my heart."

We should be just as liberal with praise in our friendships as we are in our marriages and parenting. It is likely that verbal messages of love and acceptance will touch our friends significantly because adults do not often hear words of praise from adults outside the family circle.

————————

*Today I will bless a friend with a word of appreciation.*

*Your love to me was wonderful.*
—2 SAM. 1:26

David would always look back on his friendship with Jonathan as one of the best things in his life. Friends who praise us and value us highly are rare, indeed.

David and Jonathan had promised to be friends for life. Even though they were not able to be together long, they remained actively committed to one another—a commitment that carried over to the next generation.

Years later, after Jonathan had died in battle and David had become king, David summoned Jonathan's grown son, Mephibosheth, to the palace. In appreciation for all the many kindnesses Jonathan had shown him, David restored the young man's lost inheritance and treated him as his own son.

True friendship is a series of kindnesses. As James Boswell said, "We cannot tell the precise moment when friendship is formed. As in filling a vessel drop by drop, there is at last a drop which makes it run over; so in a series of kindnesses there is at last one which makes the heart run over."

*How can I bless a friend with an act of kindness?*

*A man who has friends must himself
be friendly.* —PROV. 18:24

What kind of friend are you? Reflecting on that question, Marcia was amazed to think about how she had grown as a friend. Having moved frequently when she was growing up, she knew how to be friendly. She found it relatively easy to introduce herself to strangers and start a conversation. But it was only in the last few years that she had learned to cultivate deep friendships.

She learned by watching others, and by receiving care and affection from many wonderful women. Some were older women, some younger. Their age didn't seem to matter. The one thing they had in common was drawing from the Source of Blessing. The love they shared was an overflow of the love God poured into their hearts.

There was Norma, so effusive with her hugs. Molly, gentle Molly, the patient listener who was so attentive. And Monica, who always sent uplifting cards of praise. (What a gift when she'd had a rotten day!) Then there was Mary Ellen, who challenged her to reach for the best in herself.

She'd had many teachers. And even now, as she was teaching others, she was still learning.

*May I always be a perpetual learner in the school of friendship.*

> *You will receive a rich welcome.*
> —2 PETER 1:11 NIV

Meaningful touch, the first element of the blessing, that is so instrumental in communicating parental acceptance to a child or enriching a marriage, also plays a big part in deepening friendships.

On Christmas Eve, Diane and Marty went to two church services—one across town and one at their own church. They had always wondered about that large, impressive church and when friends asked them to go, they thought it would be an interesting experience. It was. The hymns resounded richly in the cathedral-like sanctuary; the stained-glass windows were beautiful. But Diane felt a coldness there as everyone stood stoically with their arms down by their side.

After that service, they went to the informal service at their own small church. The first person to greet them was Amanda, who gathered Diane up in her arms as soon as she saw her. Her own mother couldn't have hugged her more warmly! Amanda's arms were always opened wide, but that night Diane appreciated her expression of friendship more than ever.

*Let my body welcome friendship.*

*Greet one another with a kiss of love.*
—1 PETER 5:14

Our bodies do speak. A gentle touch, a kiss, a hug, are all tangible expressions of what is in our hearts. Of course, if we hugged and kissed everyone, touch would be meaningless! This kind of outward demonstration of affection is reserved for significant people in our lives. Touch becomes meaningful when the toucher, desiring to bless, reaches out for the other's benefit, not personal satisfaction.

To stand or sit near the person to whom we are speaking and to use frequent body contact communicates closeness. There are ways we can show we value both the person speaking and the person's words. Who doesn't want to be listened to with rapt attention!

There are times when loving touch can take on greater meaning. To sit with a friend in grief and put a comforting arm around her can communicate closeness in a way that words can't. "I'm sorry," the loving arm seems to say, "I'm hurting because you are hurting. Let me share your pain."

*Say it with touch, "I care."*

> *Shall I come to you with a rod, or in love and a
> spirit of gentleness?*
> —1 COR. 4:21

When reaching out to our friends through touch, even with a loving heart, it is good to consider a word of caution.

We live in a society that has so abused the gentle art of touching that many people are afraid to be touched. For adults from abusive homes, any touch, however well-intended, can be emotionally laden with hurtful memories.

Some people, though never abused, feel better with space around themselves. Being in tune with a friend's comfort zone prevents touch that may appear threatening.

JoEllen was once surprised by two youth pastors who grabbed her in a double bear hug. JoEllen, who was raised by parents who never touched her at all, panicked and pushed them away.

Later, JoEllen was fortunate to find several close friends who were sensitive in communicating warmth through touch. In their gentle hugs and soft touches of affection, she relaxed and learned to hug back.

*I will be respectful of my friends' boundaries.*

*Be kind and compassionate to one another.*
—EPH. 4:32 NIV

Touch can be a blessed assurance that we are not alone. Even when friendships threaten to fracture and fall to pieces, touch can be an important symbol of the tie that binds.

For years Wendy had gone to the same church and made several deep friendships. An older friend, Thelma, felt very upset when Wendy moved to another church. Wendy assured her that she wasn't moving out of town, just changing churches. They would still see each other.

Thelma was hurt and angry. Even though, in her head, she understood what Wendy was saying, in her heart, she felt abandoned. "People always leave me," Thelma said, confronting Wendy.

"I'm not leaving you," Wendy said, though she knew that words alone would not assure Thelma.

To let Thelma know in a nonverbal way that Wendy valued their friendship, Wendy touched Thelma's arm as they talked. This helped Wendy withstand Thelma's anger and it assured Thelma with a sense of "I care about you. I will not let you go."

Thelma got the message. Gradually, she felt free to say goodbye to Wendy without saying goodbye to their relationship.

---

*Touch helps us to hold on to one another.*

> *If an enemy were insulting me, I could endure it;*
> *. . . . but it is you, a man like myself, my*
> *companion, my close friend.* —PS. 55:12–14 NIV

Touch can restore and heal even the most hurtful things that happen in friendships.

Because we invest so much of ourselves in friendships, we can harbor the pain of a broken relationship for years. In Joan's case, she still carried hurt from forty years ago when two close missionary friends worked behind her back to get her sent home from the country where they'd served together.

Joan still could not forgive them and the bitterness from that hidden wound seemed to poison her ministry. She wanted to be cleansed from it.

Sue, a friend who was praying with her about this, felt led to wash Joan's feet. Massaging her feet in a basin of warm, fragranced water, Sue expressed Jesus' love for her. The water in the basin seemed to represent all the tears Joan had poured out during the years. Jesus' tears were mingled with hers.

Sue spoke words of confession for the friends who had betrayed Joan. "Joan, forgive us. We didn't know what we were doing."

Touched by Jesus' love, Joan was able to see past her hurt and freely forgive. In that moment, she felt like a new woman.

---

*There is healing in Your hands.*

*Then He said to Thomas, "Reach your finger here, and look at My hands; and reach your hand here, and put it into My side. Do not be unbelieving, but believing."*

—JOHN 20:27

Several weeks after Joan's foot-washing experience, Sue received a jubilant letter from her friend. "The hurt is truly gone! In a new way I am touching the Lord, whom I have loved as long as I can remember." This was an amazing statement for a seventy-year-old missionary.

Blessing our friends through touch can affirm, support, and heal. But even more than that, it can convey the touch of Jesus, our truest Friend.

Jesus brought the kingdom of love to people by physically touching them two thousand years ago. He longs to be as real to us now as He was then. When we minister to our friends through human touch we embody the love of Christ and put them in touch with Him.

"Do you not know that your body is the temple of the Holy Spirit?" asked Paul. "Therefore glorify God in your body. . ." (1 Cor. 6:19–20). What greater way can we glorify God than by taking a hand or giving an embrace to extend His love to a friend?

*Through you, a friend can feel His touch.*

*I have called you friends, for all things that I heard
from My Father I have made known to you.*
—JOHN 15:15

Jesus valued friendship highly. Even though He
moved among crowds of people, most of His time was
spent in the company of a few close friends. These
friendships deepened as He shared His heart with
them.

To share our thoughts and feelings is probably the
reason most of us choose friends. Women look for a
friend to whom they can tell anything; someone they
can trust with their secrets.

Even though men frequently look for friends with
whom to share activities rather than secrets, they do
have this need too. In a national study for *Playboy*
magazine, men were asked what qualities they seek
in an ideal lover. Surprisingly, sexual attraction ranked
far down on the list. The majority of men were looking
for someone with whom they could be totally open and
honest.

We all yearn for intimacy. Friendship is a place of
blessing, a safe place, where we can be open and vulnerable; a place where two people can show how
much they value one another by giving the gift of
themselves.

_____

*Lord, thank You that I can trust another with my heart secrets.*

> *Accept one another, then, just as Christ accepted you.*
>                                              —ROM. 15:7 NIV

Sometimes we keep secrets from ourselves. A deep secret many women hide from others and themselves is that they do not love or accept who they are.

Even the most competent and successful-looking woman can feel this way. There are many reasons for this. A woman who, as a child, did not receive parental acceptance always hungers for the unconditional love she missed. Women who have a solid self-esteem can still experience feelings of low self-worth when hit by a crisis: divorce, the loss of a job, the loss of a loved one, or any broken relationship.

At times like this, the affirming words of a friend can be worth a basket of gold. Imagine how uplifting it was for a woman, who was feeling down, to receive this card from a friend: "I wanted to send you this note to express my appreciation, love, and admiration for you—your person, so dear; your gifts, so many and varied; your friendship, a treasure."

---

*Is there a friend I should affirm today?*

*A word spoken in due season, how good it is!*
—PROV. 15:23

In many households it is Mom who is careful to praise and build up other members of the family. She is more likely to compliment her husband on his tie than he is to praise what she is wearing. And her children, whom she may affirm daily, don't always think of affirming her.

The only person who often thinks to affirm Mom is another mom! For this reason, the second element of the blessing, verbal praise, is particularly meaningful to women friends.

Pam, an attractive blonde, brightens up as she greets a friend she hasn't seen for awhile. "Terry, you look great! Your hair is beautiful—and those colors look wonderful on you!" The two women, wearing jeans, are meeting in another friend's kitchen, but Pam's compliment makes her friend feel like Cinderella dressed for the ball!

Moms, who are on the dishing-out side of compliments, are, themselves, sometimes starved for a compliments. How they savor a word of praise!

*Lord, remind me to nourish my friends with praise.*

*Well done, good and faithful servant.*
—MATT. 25:21

Many women grow up feeling incompetent. Society is doing its best to build confidence in women. Girl Scout troups visit hi-tech/science fairs and talk to women engineers; articles abound telling parents how they can build self-esteem in their daughters. Still, when it comes to doing any kind of job, women tend to feel under-rated and need to feel appreciated.

Carla came in dragging, weighted down with a load of groceries. When she flipped on the telephone answering machine, a cheerful voice rang out: "I just want you to know how tender and loving your leadership was last night. You did a magnificent job!" Carla smiled. It was Jean, a friend who had attended the prayer vigil Carla led last night at church. What a boost Jean's compliment was!

Have you ever told a mom she's doing a great job raising her children? She looks amazed. She is astonished that anyone notices! And yet, parenting is a highly skilled, challenging occupation that requires great creativity and energy to be done right.

Successful parenting deserves a standing ovation.

---

*"Good job!" Say it to a friend.*

> *And the desert shall rejoice and blossom as the
> rose.*
> —ISA. 35:1

A friend's affirming words can be deeply refreshing
to someone whose heart is parched from a lifetime of
living without blessing words.

Some wives have husbands who find it difficult to
verbally express affection. "My wife knows I love her,"
husbands reason. "Why should I tell her over and
over?" Other wives have husbands, absorbed in work
or hobbies, who simply aren't there to say the words
they need to hear.

Most women have an emotional need to hear that
they are loved, and they need to hear those words
again and again. Other women know this. The sensitive friend of a lonely wife can do a lot to provide the
words of affirmation that are missing at home.

Other women may have grown up in homes where
their parents withheld words of love and acceptance.
Words of appreciation from a loving friend can help fill
that empty love tank that was never filled by nurturing
parents.

"I love you! You mean so much to me!" are words
of blessing that nourish a friendship and make it bloom
and grow.

*May my words be a refreshment to a thirsty friend.*

*My purpose is that they be encouraged in heart and united in love.* —COL. 2:2 NIV

A powerful way to celebrate and strengthen the special bond that friends share is to speak affirming words along with a word picture.

One friend sent another a card with a spreading oak on the front. Under the oak were the words, "Your friendship is a sheltering tree." It reminded both friends of all the time they'd spent sitting together under trees sharing their deepest feelings. Every time they looked at an oak like that, it reminded them of their friendship.

Another woman sent her friend a card with two small children splashing in the ocean. On the front were the words, "Summer afternoon, summer afternoon; to me those have always been the two most beautiful words in the English language" (Henry James). Inside, the card read, "Nothing can compare with the friendship we share." This visual image reminded both women of the times they spent laughing together and having fun. It was also a reminder that no matter how busy they were, they needed to take time to play.

*How do you picture your friendships?*

> *And when they had opened their treasures, they*
> *presented gifts to Him: gold, frankincense, and*
> *myrrh.*
> —MATT. 2:11

Gift-giving is a wonderful way to show we value our friends. Just as the wise men honored Jesus with their gifts, so we honor our friends when we give them a gift, a tangible expression of our love.

Cindy and Darlene were close friends. One of their favorite activities was walking around a lake sharing their thoughts and feelings. One day as they sat down on a bench, Darlene said, "I have something for you."

Darlene handed Cindy a beautifully wrapped gift, an early birthday present. As always, Darlene had taken great care in picking just the right wrapping. She had also written a tender card that expressed her love. When Cindy opened the gift, she was so touched she couldn't speak. It was a calendar of gorgeous seascape photographs. Cindy had confided that she loved to picture herself walking beside the ocean with Jesus during her devotional times.

Cindy was overwhelmed. Darlene had given her many gifts, but this one was special. She couldn't believe she had a friend who knew her so well and could share what most deeply touched her heart.

*My friend is such a gift to me. Is there something I can give her?*

*Oh, that I had one to hear me!*
—JOB 31:35

$A$s with our spouses and our children, one of the greatest gifts we can give our friends is to listen.

People are literally dying for lack of someone to listen to them. Studies have shown that lonely people live shorter lives than the general population. Living in isolation is dangerous to physical and emotional health because people living alone tend to not take care of themselves. Why should they? Neglected by others, lonely people often neglect themselves.

Cut off from others, it is easy to be sucked into a downward spiral of loneliness. A divorcée, mother of two, goes up to bed alone. Her children are with their father and his new live-in partner. The house feels like a tomb. She reaches for sleeping pills, thinking what difference would it make if she took too many. She hesitates, then reaches for the phone. "If you need me," her friend has said, "call at anytime even, if it's just to talk." And once again, "just talking," knowing someone else understands, is enough to turn her attitude around from despair to hope.

*Lord, help me to be attentive to friends who need a listening ear, and help me to reach out to others and to You when I am in need.*

*Whoever shuts his ears to the cry of the poor will also cry himself and not be heard.* —PROV. 21:13

How flattered we feel when someone genuinely listens to us, giving us undivided attention.

One woman sent her friend a card that said, "God gives people ears so they can hear, but you are special . . . because you listen. Thank you."

Another woman poured out her feelings about a problem, then paused to tell her friend how much she appreciated her careful attention. "You're all ear," the woman said amazed. "It's as if your whole body is an ear!"

Listening, by itself, can be therapeutic. You don't have to be a trained professional to listen with love. A friend's listening ear can act as a sounding board to help us clarify thoughts, try out new ideas or see things from a different point of view. "You don't have to fix the problem," one friend assured another, "it just feels good to know you understand."

Learning to listen is one of the surest ways to deepen a friendship. "The road to the heart is the ear," wrote Voltaire.

*Lord, forgive me if I have not been responsive to a friend crying out to be heard.*

*You have loosed my bonds.*
—PS. 116:16

Loving friends can often see potential in us that God can bless and use in the future. For this reason, they can be very instrumental in applying the fourth element of the blessing, picturing a special future.

Alan was an old friend of Jeanette's whom she hadn't seen for years. When he came back to church after a long absence, Jeannette was saddened to learn that Alan's wife had left him for another man. Alan was still stuck in his pain.

People at church asked Jeannette if she could speak to Alan. All he could talk about, they said, was the divorce. When he was introduced to new people, it was the first thing he told them about.

Gently, Jeanette tried to show Alan how much he was limiting himself. "Alan, it's as if you have a sign around your neck, 'Divorced.' There's much more to you than that. You are talented and gifted." Over time, with Jeanette's encouragement, Alan began to think of himself as someone of value with something to give, not just a cast off to be pitied. Released from the limits of the past, Alan felt free to grow and change.

*Lord, help me to be an encouragement to my friends and affirm their potential.*

*Love will cover a multitude of sins.*
—1 PETER 4:8

A friend who listens with love is not judgmental. "There is no terror like that of being known," wrote Ralph Waldo Emerson. Most of us are afraid to share our innermost selves with others because we fear rejection. "If my friend knew that about me, she wouldn't think so highly of me," we tell ourselves. "In fact, she might walk away!"

Surprisingly, we may find that a good friend is more understanding than we think. This was the quality Coleen admired most in her friend. "Evie didn't flinch when I told her about my sinful past. I didn't detect a trace of judgment or condemnation. It was so freeing."

A loving friend knows us through and through. We can confide the worst thing we have done, and she will still accept us. This acceptance not only releases us from the emotional stress of trying to be something we are not, but also frees us to explore our shadow side, which is as much a part of us as the things we are proud of.

We bless our friends when we listen with compassion and accept their weaknesses as well as strengths.

---

*Lord, teach me to be wholly accepting of my friends, as You are.*

*Open your hearts to us.*
—2 COR. 7:2

A caring listener opens her heart, as well as her ear, to a friend, listening between the lines to what is not said as well as what is said; sensitive to body language as well as spoken words.

Kendra was this kind of listener. She had been praying for a big project that another friend, Pat, was taking on. Pat took her out to lunch to show her appreciation for Kendra's support and friendship. Pat was cheerful, but shared that the lead she had hoped would get the project off the ground had not materialized.

"How do you feel about it?" asked Kendra.

Pat tried to be honest. "Still hopeful. I'll just have to wait for God to open another door."

Kendra must have sensed her disappointment. A few days later, Pat received an understanding note from her friend. "You know in your head that another door will open. I pray that you'll feel this way in your heart as well."

Kendra was able to put into words what Pat was not able to say. Pat knew that when she fully let go of that disappointment it would be because of the prayers of a discerning friend.

―――――――――

*Today I will listen between the lines to discern a need my friend might have.*

> *Your faithfulness reaches to the clouds.*
> —PS. 36:5

Sometimes when we picture our own future, we limit ourselves, and we also limit God. Friends can help broaden our vision.

Joyce listened as Marni shared her frustrations about starting a mid-life career. Marni loved Christian work, but couldn't make a living doing it. She was trying to find a way to have a part-time money-making job while still doing ministry on the side. "Not to do ministry," said Marni, "would cut my heart out."

Joyce wrote her a candid note. "What I heard you really saying was: 1) if you were a man, 2) if you were younger, 3) if you were not semi-retired into motherhood . . . you might be called to the ministry. So, are you being called? Have you ever considered going to seminary? You already have a pastor's heart and a healing touch. Are you putting limitations on where God might be leading? I'd like to encourage you to think outside the box we women sometimes place around ourselves."

Joyce's challenging words exploded the parameters of Marni's thinking and opened up a whole new world of possibilities.

---

*Do you have a friend who feels boxed in? Can you help her break out of that box?*

> *By faith the walls of Jericho fell down.*
> —HEB. 11:30

Picturing a special future for our friends can be transforming.

Regina grew up in an alcoholic family. To protect herself from her parents' abuse, she built a thick wall around herself. She built the wall to keep them out, but later in life, when she no longer needed that protection, her defenses kept other people out too, even people she loved.

In Gloria Evan's parable, *The Wall,* a loving friend throws a flower over the wall of a lonely woman and helps her see how to dismantle her defenses. This is what happened to Regina. She had a friend who won her trust and little by little her defenses came tumbling down.

"Some day," said Barb, "you will be the one who throws flowers over other people's walls."

Five years later, Barb was delighted to receive this letter from Regina: "Years ago, you tried to tell me I was special. I'm beginning to believe that. I caught hold of your vision and I'm learning to minister to women as you do."

A new vision. A new woman. All because one woman saw the potential hidden in another.

*Lord, give me eyes to see hidden possibilities in my friends.*

> *For which of you, intending to build a tower, does not sit down first and count the cost.*
>
> —LUKE 14:28

It is one thing to picture a special future for a friend, it is another to make a wholehearted commitment to seeing that future come to pass. The final element of bestowing the blessing, active commitment, takes staying power and sacrifice.

Yesterday we read about a friend reaching out to another woman who, in turn, was empowered to reach out to others. That kind of change did not come easily. Barb met with Regina for a couple of hours every week for two years. She listened to Regina pour out her pain, encouraged her and built her up when she felt down, verbally praised her strengths and comforted her when there were setbacks. When Regina moved out of town, Barb continued to write letters of encouragement and to be available by phone.

Commitment is costly. It takes time, energy, resources, and a conscious decision to put people first; but the investment brings rich rewards. "We take care of our health," wrote Ralph Waldo Emerson, "we lay up money, we make our rooms tight, and our clothing sufficient; but who provides wisely that he shall not be wanting in the best property of all—friends?"

*Investing in friends brings rich rewards.*

*A friend loves at all times, and a brother is born
for adversity.*
                                    —PROV. 17:17

Friends usually come together because they have
something in common: perhaps they were college
roommates, now serve on PTA together, or share a
concern in the neighborhood. One common bond
deepens friendships like no other—adversity.

Two schoolteachers discover they have both gone
through the same crisis, having a radical mastectomy.
Boosting each other's spirits, they make light of a dev-
astating operation by calling each other "bosom buddies."

A couple of moms who are friends suddenly grow
closer as they share the same turmoil, going through
mid-life divorce. One invites the other to move in during the transition; the other cares for the children
while her friend takes a much needed vacation. To
grow stronger through the crisis, they recommend
counselors and support groups to each other.

Life experience draws friends close for support and
guidance.

*How I cherish the friends I've made through hard times.*

> *Two are better than one . . . but woe to him who
> is alone when he falls, for he has no one to help
> him up.*
> —ECCL. 4:9–10

Within a few weeks of Eleanor's losing her husband,
Bea's husband also died. Sundays were particularly
painful for Eleanor because she had always reserved
that day for time alone with her husband. Sunday was
*their* day; it was torturous to get through that day
alone.

Sensing this, Bea invited Eleanor to a Sunday singles' meeting at a local church. A nice thought, Eleanor said, but she had another commitment. Bea
invited her again, but Eleanor couldn't go then either.
The third time Bea asked, Eleanor felt she had to confess the truth: "Bea, the last thing I want to do is go to
a singles' event."

Bea was persistent. Just go once, she suggested. If
Eleanor didn't like it, Bea promised never to ask again.
Eleanor went to please her friend, but was surprised
to find how much she enjoyed herself. It wasn't at all
what she had expected. The evening was a low-key,
fun time of singing, prayer, fellowship, and a helpful
talk. It was exactly what Eleanor needed to get
through her Sunday blues. Thirteen years later, she is
still going!

---

*Sometimes it is not easy to bless a friend in need, but don't give up
right away.*

> *As iron sharpens iron, so a man sharpens the*
> *countenance of his friend.*
> —PROV. 27:17

Crises can be great catalysts to growth. Close friends also give each other permission to continue to spur each other on to growth and maturity by regularly offering feedback and sometimes loving correction. This sharpening process is called accountability.

Gary and I (John) give each other the freedom to hold one another accountable, perhaps to point out an attitude that needs adjusting, or to ask a hard question that needs to be asked. We also have key friends across the country who can call us at any time to see if our lives are staying in Christlike balance and moving in the right direction.

Accountability is love that cares enough to confront. "It isn't easy when my friend says something candid that I'd rather not hear," a woman reflects. "But we've been friends a long time. My friend knows me well and loves me so deeply that I take to heart whatever she says. Over the years, her insightful comments have been extremely helpful to mold and shape who I am."

*Lord, thank You for friends who are willing to say hard things.*

> *Give, and it will be given to you: good measure,*
> *pressed down, shaken together, and running over.*
> —LUKE 6:38

Seeds of blessing sown in friendship are productive beyond measure. A friendship of long duration grows stronger as both friends give and receive, laugh and cry, mutually encourage and support one another, and challenge each other to greater growth.

Joanne sent her friend a card that captured the fullness of their friendship. It showed four pictures of a tree as it progressed through the seasons: first, resplendent with summer foliage; then, losing its fall leaves; bare in winter; and finally, leafing out again in a beautiful spring green. The caption under the pictures read, "We have changed . . . our lives have changed . . . our love is not the same . . . it's even stronger."

Joanne and Jane had been through many seasons of change. There had been times of joyful celebration, times of tears, times of stretching, times of testing, times of trusting each other with the truth. Like Jonathan and David, they were lifelong friends. Their commitment to one another was something they could count on, something that blessed them both.

---

*Oh, Lord, how I praise You for close companions who journey with me along the path of life.*

*May the Lord make you increase and abound in love to one another and to all.* —1 THESS. 3:12

God's blessing is a gift that keeps on giving. When we receive the blessing and learn to share it with family and friends, it continues to flow on beyond the bounds of those close to us, touching church family, neighbors, peers and colleagues, casual acquaintances.

Our first priority should be to give all the elements of the blessing on a regular basis to our husbands, children, and parents and friends. But other people cross our path whom God also wants to bless through us. When you chat with the clerk at the grocery store, or take a letter from your mail carrier, or give a book to the librarian, ask yourself, "What can I do to give at least one element of the blessing to this person?" It may be just a smile or a friendly word of encouragement, but what a difference it will make to their day!

Because the Source of blessing constantly pours out His love to us, we can pass that blessing on to others. "Freely you have received," said Jesus, "freely give" (Matt. 10:8).

*Lord, make me a blessing to others today.*

> *She is a tree of life to those who embrace her; those who lay hold of her will be blessed.*
> —PROV. 3:18 NIV

Women, mothers especially, are uniquely equipped to bless others. Physically made to carry and nurse babies, emotionally very relationship-oriented, women are natural nurturers. They can sense the needs of those around them and have a longing to respond.

In Aramaic, the language Jesus spoke, the word *compassion* comes from the root word for "womb." From the early months of pregnancy when an expecting mom can feel a little body moving mysteriously within her own, in deep and silent intimacy, to the first cries of an infant making her breasts fill with milk, a new mother feels deeply connected with another human being.

This intimate link between mother and child births more than compassion for her immediate family. A new mother may find she has a heightened empathy for other families as well as for her own. Her compassion may move her to help a needy family down the street or across the world.

---

*Thank You, heavenly Father, for equipping me as a mother to bless others.*

*Therefore, as we have opportunity, let us do good
to all, especially to those who are of the household
of faith.*
                                              —GAL. 6:10

Beyond the inner circle of our own family and
friends, our next priority should be to bless the family
of believers. When we accept Christ, we are adopted
into His spiritual family fleshed out in the local church.

What does it mean to be part of a church family? It
means that each individual is to be highly valued, but
that, together, we are even more valuable.

At Pam's church on Thanksgiving, the congregation
got together to praise God for their life as a body.
When Pam stood up, she told everyone about the special Thanksgiving soup that her daughter had helped
prepare at preschool. Every child took in a vegetable,
peeled it, and cut it up for the soup. The soup then
simmered for hours. The next day, family and friends
were invited to share in the feast.

"Our church is like that Thanksgiving soup," said
Pam. "We are all different, like potatoes, carrots, and
green beans. We are not very flavorful on our own, but
when stripped down, cut up, and stewed together with
love, our flavors mingle and we give off a heavenly
aroma—the aroma of Christ."

*Lord, teach me to highly value every member of my church family.*

*But now indeed there are many members, yet one body. And the eye cannot say to the hand, "I have no need of you."* —1 COR. 12:20–21

One member of our church family is not to be held higher than another. But of course we are all human and inequalities do occur. The blessing is a wonderful tool to help prevent this from happening.

Vicky knew that Geoff, one of the church janitors, suffered from low self-esteem. She affirmed him by touching him lightly on the shoulder and praising him verbally whenever she could.

One day Geoff said he had seen a magazine article about her posted in the church office. Geoff was impressed. "Did you really write six books?"

Vicky downplayed her accomplishments, sensing that Geoff was putting her on a pedestal.

How could she show him how much she valued him? Vicky noticed a picture in the nursery where they were talking. It showed Jesus looking lovingly at a circle of children. She picked up the painting and showed it to Geoff. "Geoff, in His eyes, we are all special."

A shy smile softened Geoff's face. He understood. "Hey, looks like I'm going to get the HUD house I applied for. Want to come over for dinner?"

"I'd like that," said Vicky.

*We need each other.*

*Now you are the body of Christ, and each one of
you is a part of it.*          —1 COR. 12:27 NIV

To truly reflect the oneness that Christ envisioned for
the church, we have to be deeply committed to one
another. The blessing, practiced rightly, can provide
the glue that binds us together when hurt, however
slight, could tear apart the fabric of the body.

Brianne, a regular at a mothers' support group, was
surprised to see a woman she had seen at church, but
never at the group. "I didn't know you had children,"
Brianne commented.

"I don't," said Ellen with an awkward smile. "I just
came to get to know people."

Brianne sensed that her comment had offended Ellen. She leaned over and put her hand on Ellen's arm.
"I'm sorry I said that. I'm glad you came."

A few days later, on Sunday, Ellen came up to Brianne. "Thank you for being so sensitive the other day.
People do say that and it bothers me. No one has ever
apologized for making that comment."

Brianne discovered that Ellen struggled with infertil-
ity. Brianne's comment hit that tender nerve. The experience, which could have driven them apart, drew
Brianne and Ellen close as friends.

*When it comes to repairing torn hearts an old adage applies: "A
stitch in time saves nine."*

> *By this all will know that you are My disciples, if*
> *you have love for one another.* —JOHN 13:35

Church should be a caring community—a place where we can cultivate the deep relationships we hunger for. But sometimes that is asking a lot.

Shirley was fifty-five, a warm and outgoing church leader whom Linda, a young Christian, admired. At a church retreat they were asked to cut out magazine pictures that revealed something about themselves, paste the pictures on a paper plate, and hang the plate around their necks.

Shirley pasted a big padlock on her plate. "What does that mean?" Linda asked in surprise.

"I'm a member of the padlocked generation," said Shirley. As tears came to her eyes, she confided how hard it was for her to share her thoughts and feelings with others.

Linda was amazed. She would never have guessed Shirley's struggle.

Like many people inside the church, as well as outside, Shirley had never received the blessing. By becoming a listening and affirming friend, Linda was able to provide the blessing Shirley had missed. That was the key that unlocked this seemingly confident woman's heart.

*Oh Lord, teach us to value vulnerability.*

*Pray for one another, that you may be healed.*
—JAMES 5:16

Sometimes blessing others takes courage. Sara was part of a Bible study group that wanted to put the Bible into practice. Taking the command to pray for one another seriously, they decided to go to the hospital and pray for a ninety-year-old man from their congregation who had had a cerebral hemorrhage.

Driving to the hospital, Sara began to get cold feet. How would they explain to Carl what they wanted to do? Would his roommate be offended when he heard them praying out loud?

Carl looked surprised when eight young people he didn't know walked into his room. After some small talk, Jim asked if they could pray for him.

Carl smiled broadly. "Oh, sure. Just like it says in James!"

Everyone gathered around Carl's bed, gently touching him, as Jesus had laid hands on the sick, and prayed out loud.

Carl was effusive and thanked everyone for coming. As they were leaving, Sara noticed a sign on the end of Carl's roommate's bed saying the man was deaf. He hadn't been offended at all!

---

*Holy Spirit, empower me to risk reaching out.*

> *Weeping may endure for a night, but joy comes in
> the morning.*
> —PS. 30:5

Praying for Carl had been a mountaintop experience
for Sara. Carl looked so well when they left, Sara was
sure he was instantly healed.

She was stunned the next day when she found out
Carl was paralyzed; he couldn't even speak or lift his
head. Sara's heart sank. Why would God lead her and
her friends to act on His promises, then seem to let
them down? She was angry, bitter, and confused. But
she kept on praying, and so did the others.

The group followed Carl's progress closely. That
week they were engaged in a tug-of-war, pleading for
Carl's life. Sara felt committed to Carl as if there were
an invisible bond between them. At the end of the
week, the doctors decided to perform a delicate operation. It was a success.

The group continued to pray for Carl, and visit him
in the hospital, as he recovered. When Carl returned
to church, Sara went to him after the service and
hugged him. She felt she had traveled a long road with
him. She was learning that active commitment to see
a blessing through was as important as spoken words
and good intentions.

---

*Lord, keep me faithful in my commitments to those I bless.*

*Now all who believed were together, and had all
things in common.*
　　　　　　　　　　　　　　　　　—ACTS 2:44

Terri smiled. Every time she read that verse, she
thought of that blue maternity dress. Half a dozen new
moms had worn it at church. She and Dan, like the
other young couples on fixed incomes, knew what it
was to be in need. All of the couples were committed
to helping each other through tough times.

She also remembered her baby coming a month
early. She and Dan were totally unprepared. The nursery was still a bare, empty room; it hadn't yet occurred
to them to buy clothes or toys or baby powder. They
assumed there would be time.

There wasn't. Terri wondered what she would do
when she got home from the hospital. She needn't
have worried.

When she came home, she found a fully stocked
nursery: complete with a crib and dresser full of carefully folded clothes, linens, everything that was
needed. Friends from church had arranged for a dia-
per service to do the laundry, and for two weeks meals
were brought over every night.

Since then, whenever someone at church had a new
baby, Terri was always the first to volunteer to take in
a meal.

_____

*Lord, help me to be aware of others' needs.*

> *For God so loved the world that He gave His only begotten Son, that whoever believes in Him should not perish but have everlasting life.* —JOHN 3:16

There are people outside the church who come from loving homes where parents have given them a partial blessing, but we believe no one can receive the full measure of the blessing without a personal relationship with Jesus Christ. The most important way a person can bless others is to lead them to the Source of Blessing Himself.

How do we lead people to Christ? Darcy was a committed Christian who wanted to share her faith but didn't know how to do it. She tried being part of an evangelism team, but the words she was supposed to say felt canned. They weren't her words and they didn't sound sincere.

At the same time, Darcy had a heart for hurting people. She had a passion to help, support, and encourage others. One day a grateful friend wrote a note which was a great encouragement to her. "You have always wanted to know how to share your faith. I believe that *you* are your faith. God in the flesh!"

*Your life is the only Bible some people will ever read.*

*They looked to Him and were radiant.*
—PS. 34:5

Have you ever known people who seem to shine from the inside out? Their inner radiance often comes from being in the presence of God. In a world that seems inky black with bad news, their very faces seem to testify to the bright light of God's love. And other people want to be near them to be blessed by their presence.

Victoria was a lay leader in her church, wrestling with challenges in ministry and feeling a lack of getting things done. In the midst of her feelings of inadequacy, a maintenance workman who worked regularly on the grounds of the townhouse complex where she lived leaned out the window of his pick-up one day and said, "You're always smiling. You must be a nice person."

This compliment from a stranger took her completely by surprise. It made her realize that no matter what she was doing, through significant ministry projects or small, everyday actions, her purpose was the same—to glorify God. And she could do this simply by being herself.

*Lord, use me in little ways as well as big ways today.*

> *I was a stranger and you took me in.*
> —MATT. 25:35

In our neighborhoods, opportunities abound for us to bless others. A company wife is uprooted and moved across the country. She's a stranger trying to settle her children into a new school and learn her way around the community. Divorce leaves a neighbor suddenly excluded from parties and outings. She now feels like an outsider, a stranger.

In our highly mobile, fractured society, we can bless others with the gift of acceptance by offering them a sense of belonging and inclusion.

Zoey had a neighbor who was newly divorced. On the spur of the moment, she invited Sylvia to a volley-ball social. Sylvia said she'd like to go, then called back again. "Zoey, thanks for including me," she said. "It meant a lot."

Zoey was surprised. She didn't have time to spend hours helping her neighbor as she'd like to, but this small invitation was one manageable way she could reach out.

Sylvia had told her how empty the house was when the children were gone, how cut off she felt from family and friends. It was one rejection after another. How wonderful to be able to include others instead of shutting them out!

---

*Are there strangers you know who could be included in some of your activities?*

*You shall love your neighbor as yourself.*
—MARK 12:31

It is easy to love neighbors who are congenial, but what about a neighbor who lashes out in anger?

Liz could not believe that the vociferous person on the phone was Edith, a demure neighbor. As head of the neighborhood association, Liz's husband had to inform Edith that her estate sale was an infringement of an association bylaw.

When Liz picked up the phone and heard Edith screaming, she was stunned. She knew that Edith had just lost her husband in a tragic accident a few weeks before. Liz had wanted to reach out and offer help, but had never gotten around to it. When Edith accused the neighborhood of not caring, it struck a chord.

Liz felt she owed Edith an apology for not showing her concern. The next day, Liz showed up on Edith's doorstep with a rose. Liz didn't know what to expect. Would Edith still be angry?

When Edith opened the door, she looked embarrassed. She was the first to apologize. Liz listened to Edith's pain and both women hugged. Liz came as a neighbor, but left a friend.

---

*Obedience opens the door for God to work.*

## October 15 – BLESSERS, UNITE!

*Again I say to you that if two of you agree on earth concerning anything that they ask, it will be done for them by My Father in heaven.* —MATT. 18:19

Janet felt called to be a source of blessing to her neighborhood school. During her devotional time one morning, God asked her to increase her prayer life. The next day, Janet heard a radio interview with the director of *Moms-In-Touch,* a national organization of Christian moms who meet in homes to pray for their local schools. She also learned that a group was starting up, the following week, for Janet's school. She was excited to join the group. Weekly, she met with other mothers to pray for teachers, the administration, and children, by name.

Janet had already learned to apply the elements of the family blessing at home. She decided to use those same principles to bless people at school. Once a month, she took treats to a teacher, a janitor, or a bus driver, along with a cheerful note of encouragement and praise.

Did the prayers of these concerned moms make a difference? "We've had a fabulous response," said Janet. "One teacher called to say he knew something was different at school this year, a better tone, something he couldn't put his finger on. When he found out about us, he said, he wondered if that was it!"

*Blessers, unite! There is more power in prayer together.*

*Blessed are you among women, and blessed is the fruit of your womb!*
                              —LUKE 1:42

Volunteering at the local school is a great way to bless children by expressing high value for them and active commitment.

Marlo loved books and decided she would volunteer to read to kindergartners in the school library once a week. She enjoyed it as much as the children did, but one day it occurred to her that she could do more than read books.

One little boy named Jason was a troublemaker in the classroom, but listened attentively to Marlo read. After their reading time, Jason would come up and hold Marlo's hand. His warm affection surprised her. "Does your mom read to you at home?"

"Naw," he shrugged his shoulders. "She doesn't have time. She comes home from work when I'm in bed and she's too tired."

Marlo realized Jason was hungry for the blessing, which is every child's due. So she began to consciously bless Jason with meaningful touch (rustling his hair) and verbal encouragement. Intead of job-sharing, she saw herself as "blessing-sharing" with a mom who could not fulfill that need in her own son's life.

---

*Giving the blessing is a job we all can share in.*

*The earth is full of his unfailing love.*
—PS. 33:5 NIV

Julia loved being involved in church activities, and spending hours in prayer with Christian friends. Her life-style changed, however, when she went back to work full-time.

Instead of the warmth of church, the atmosphere at work felt cold and competitive. As a salesperson in an upscale department store, her days were spent scrambling to make quotas and developing a lucrative customer base.

Julia looked forward to the day when she no longer had to work, until a Christian friend suggested she be a source of blessing right where she was—in the workplace.

So she did. God's love filled the *whole* earth. Surely it could be felt in a department store as well as in a church building. Julia began to bless the women she worked with, affirming them and offering words of encouragement. She always had a warm hug when someone had a low day. One by one, her workmates sought her out and asked why she was so cheerful. She told them about Jesus, the source of her joy, an opportunity she never would have had if she had remained a cloistered Christian.

*Bloom where you're planted!*

> *If a brother or sister is naked and destitute of daily food, and one of you says to them, "Depart in peace, be warmed and filled," but you do not give them the things which are needed for the body, what does it profit?"*
> —JAMES 2:15–16

James is right," said Essie. "How can you see someone in need, wish them a good day, and send them on their way? If you are truly interested, you'll show your care for them."

Essie is a college teacher who takes her faith into the classroom even though she can't speak openly about her religious views. She believes all students can learn, but often their backgrounds handicap them. Many have not been blessed by parents or teachers to encourage them and make the commitment to see them succeed.

So Essie offers that blessing. When she learned of one student who was suicidal, Essie visited her in the hospital. The student was facing personal problems that made life seem not worth living. Essie told her God loved her; to show her concern she called the student every day for weeks and invited her to Thanksgiving dinner.

Another student was flunking courses because she could not write. Essie made a commitment to meet with her once a week to help with her papers.

"I just see something that needs to be done," says Essie, "and do it."

*Lord, help me to put blessing into action.*

*Serve one another in love.*
—GAL. 5:13 NIV

The more creatively and wholeheartedly Christians bless others in the workplace, the stronger the statement it makes.

Ted managed eight departments in a large city hall. For twelve years, his hard-working staff had labored on a development project that finally came to fruition. Ted wanted to honor his employees in a special way to show his gratitude.

He decided to throw a party for his staff and their families, which meant inviting one hundred and fifty people to dinner. It was a considerable expense on a city employee's salary, but Ted wanted to do it. On the night of the big event, his wife was surprised to see Ted wearing a plain shirt without a tie. When she asked why he wasn't dressing up, he said, "You'll see."

Ted had arranged for the restaurant to outfit him like a waiter. He went from table to table serving his staff, then praising them in front of their families for the fine job they'd done. Ted's gesture was more than a unique way to show appreciation. It was an act of love everyone would long remember.

*Jesus, give me Your servant's heart as I learn to bless others.*

*Let us run with endurance the race that is set
before us.*
                                            —HEB. 12:1

For most of us, the call to bless others will come close
to home—within our families, neighborhoods, work-
places, and community. But some of us are called to
bless others further afield.

Cathy laughs as she remembers that hot July day
she jogged across the South Dakota prairie with four
hundred Dakota Sioux on a "Run for Sobriety," a community event designed to show support for the fight
against alcohol abuse on the reservation. "With my
blonde hair and blue eyes," Cathy says, "I stuck out like
a sore thumb, but those people are like family to me
and I want to give them hope."

Why did Cathy drive ten hours to join in the run? "I
grew up as an only child and felt isolated; out of my
pain, I see their pain of isolation."

How does she bless them? "Words don't count for
much there," says Cathy, "you have to build trust over
time." Cathy has helped market quilts the women
make and mobilized friends to fund single moms who
want to train for better jobs. Picturing a special future
and showing active commitment have been Cathy's
most effective blessing tools.

*Blessing others may take you to interesting places.*

*In you all the families of the earth shall be blessed.*
—GEN. 12:3

Paula's daughter was born six weeks premature and with pneumonia. She was purple and couldn't cry. Paula knew something was terribly wrong as nurses whisked her baby away. "If you help my child live," Paula pleaded with God, "I will commit the rest of my life to helping other children live too."

Paula's baby did miraculously pull through. That miracle was the springboard for this courageous mom's dedication to bless others. Paula immediately left her lucrative job as a special events coordinator for private corporations to assist hospitals and non-profit organizations raise funds to help children live.

Years later, on a large screen video at church, she saw pictures of a starving African mother trying to feed her child from a breast that had no milk. She felt called to go to Africa to help that mother.

Paula returns to Africa annually now and mobilizes other volunteers to get involved. "This time, as I stood in the hut of a Ugandan grandma who had taken in fifteen AIDS orphans, I was humbled to think that all of us are called to care for each other's children."

*He's got the whole world in His hands.*

*Then Jesus answered and said to her, "O woman,
great is your faith!"*
                                        —MATT. 15:28

To help empower African women to have faith in
themselves, Paula has used all the elements of the
blessing. Here are a few examples:

*Touch.* Paula arrived in a Ugandan village just after
a young mother had died. Her two small children and
several women knelt by the lifeless body and wept.
Paula did not sit on the chair provided. Kneeling and
putting her arms around one woman, Paula offered
comfort.

*Affirming words.* In return for planting crops, Ethio-
pian women were promised part of the produce. The
women were very discouraged from waiting so long
for the harvest. Paula went to the field with them, held
the dirt in her hand and smiled. "You are never closer
to the living God than when you plant things. The food
will come to feed your families."

*Picturing a special future.* Paula sends donated wedding dresses to Ugandan women who now have a wedding dress rental business. The dresses not only signify
a monogamous marriage (an important symbol of
their Christian faith), but also provide funds to help
young women be self-sufficient.

*Is there someone in my life who needs encouragement today?*

> So the LORD said to him, "What is that in your
> hand?"
> —EX. 4:2

Yesterday we read about an extraordinary woman who has a vision for empowering women around the world. Beside her, you may feel pretty ordinary.

Moses felt ordinary. When God called him to lead the Israelites out of Egypt, he thought God had the wrong person. "Who am I to take on such an assignment?"

God answered by asking a question, "What is that in your hand?"

Moses held up his shepherd's staff. A pretty ordinary tool. Then God showed him the extraordinary things He could do with that simple instrument. If Moses was willing to be used, God said, He would provide the power.

God asks us the same question. What is in your hand? What resources are at your disposal to bless others?

*The telephone.* Could you make a phone call to affirm someone? *Your house.* Could you invite a few people in for a Bible study or support group? *A day off.* Could you babysit for a young mom who longs for a much needed quiet time?

God can use anything you have in hand.

*Lord, show me the resources I have at my fingertips that can be used to bless others.*

> But as for me and my house, we will serve the
> LORD.
> —JOSH. 24:15

Norma and Wayne have literally used their house to serve the Lord.

As youth leaders in their church, they took a personal interest in one of the teenagers who came to know Christ through their ministry. They learned that Mary Anne came from an alcoholic home, a home of chaos and neglect. Norma and Wayne decided to invite Mary Anne to live with them when her parents moved out of town. Mary Anne was like a wilted plant that revived and flourished once her roots were planted in the soil of unconditional love and acceptance. Eventually, she became a missionary with an international ministry to people who had wounded pasts like her own.

Mary Anne was not the only one. Over forty years, Norma and Wayne have opened their home to many rootless teenagers who discovered the family blessing there. A plaque on Norma and Wayne's front door reads: "In this home you are loved."

What resources do you have to show Christ's love to a hurting world that lives apart from the blessing?

*How can I use my resources to serve the Lord?*

> *God loves a cheerful giver.*
> —2 COR. 9:7

Friday was Wayne's birthday. Wayne had been like a father to Mary Anne and she wanted to give this special man a meaningful gift. However, Mary Anne lived four thousands miles away and there wasn't time to send a gift so she asked her friend Sharon to help with her gift-giving.

Mary Anne knew that Wayne, a gardener, loved fresh fruit. So she wanted a basket of fruit to be sitting on the dining room table when Wayne came downstairs on his birthday. All week, Sharon worked on the arrangements. She shopped around to find just the right basket and arranged to sneak the basket into the house the night before so it would be waiting for Wayne in the morning.

Wayne was surprised and delighted. He even snapped a picture of it to send to Mary Anne. When Sharon heard this, she felt joy welling up inside of her. She thought, *That was a lot of fun. I really enjoyed surprising Wayne.*

*It really is more fun to give than receive.* She thought of all the unexpected gifts God had given her out of sheer grace and a heart of love. How much He must enjoy giving!

*Lord, thank You for sharing the joy of gift-giving with us!*

*The kingdom of heaven is like a mustard
seed . . . which indeed is the least of all seeds;
but when it is grown . . . it becomes
a tree.* —MATT. 13:31–32

As it is with faith, so it is with love. Small kindnesses,
planted like seeds over time, can produce a harvest of
blessing.

Kay wondered how she could be a support to her
mother- and father-in-law. They lived across the country and, because of illness, could not make the long
trip to see Kay's family. Kay's family could only afford
to visit once a year. This meant these loving grandparents didn't have many opportunities to enjoy their
grandchildren.

Kay decided to make a commitment. Once a week,
she would send a letter to her parents-in-law, just sharing what had been going on in the family, along with
the children's daily schoolwork.

It wasn't easy to get off a letter week after week,
but she did. She was amazed at how much her effort
meant. When they visited the grandparents, it was the
first thing they mentioned and the last. "Keep the letters coming."

The constant flow of letters and cards helped the
grandparents feel part of the family even at a distance.

---

*Small acts of kindness can bless others greatly.*

> *Look, as the clay is in the potter's hand, so are you in My hand.*
>
> —JER. 18:6

In thinking about what resources we have with which to bless others, we may overlook one of our richest—who we are.

Each of us is uniquely made by the hands of God. As the potter fashions vessels for different purposes, so God has made us with very different personalities, aptitudes, ways of relating.

If you were to list your talents and gifts, you probably would not mention the kind of person you are. And yet these intangibles can be incredible sources of blessing. For example, if you have an outgoing personality, you may be able to offer the gift of acceptance through hugs and warm words of affirmation. If you are quiet and sympathetic, you might offer the balm of listening love.

And, as a person in process, you are always on the potter's wheel, being reshaped—molded anew—each day into something even lovelier.

Are you soft and pliable, responsive to Jesus' touch? Are you in His hand? In the Word? In prayer?

————————

*Mold me, Lord, fill me, use me.*

*We are His workmanship, created in Christ Jesus
for good works, which God prepared beforehand.*
—EPH. 2:10

God's workmanship? Sometimes, looking at ourselves in despair, we wonder if God made a mistake.

Lori was big-boned and heavyset. In grade school,
she was bigger than her friends and she stuck out in
a crowd. In high school, she blamed her bigness for
lack of dates.

Then one day, on a high school career field trip,
something unexpected happened. The class was gathered around a nurse who was explaining hospital work
when a patient fell from her wheelchair. Without
thinking, Lori lifted the crying girl and put her gently
back into her chair. It would have taken two nurses
to do the job, but with Lori's size, she did it easily by
herself.

Seven years later, Lori said: "For years, I'd looked
at the way God made me as a curse, not a blessing.
But that day at the hospital, I learned that He could
use me just the way He made me! That young woman
needed my strong arms. That afternoon, for the first
time in my life, I was able to thank God for making
me big."

Today, Lori is an occupational therapist, being used
just as God made her.

*Before blessing others, we need to bless ourselves.*

*To the weak I became as weak, that I might win
the weak.*
                                    —1 COR. 9:22

God can use our weaknesses as well as our strengths,
our brokenness as well as our wholeness.

For three years, Nancy endured a terrible ordeal of
physical and emotional pain. Children who are sexually abused, as Nancy was, suffer unimaginable pain
and often have scars that stay with them for life. But
in Nancy's case, that pain brought an incredible sensitivity.

Nancy needs to be in a roomful of women for only
a few minutes to sense who among them has been
abused sexually. Without any formal training, Nancy
has a tremendously effective one-on-one counseling
ministry with women who suffer from abuse.

In much the same way, a long-time widow can comfort another who is newly grieving. A mom with a
troubled child can encourage another mom who struggles with the unexpected valleys of child-raising.

Who we are and where we've been can bless others
as we share our journeys.

*Oh Lord, thank You that You can use everything in my life, even
crippling experiences, as a blessing.*

*Jesus wept.*
—JOHN 11:35

How can you emphathize with people in pain if you've never hurt deeply yourself? Bob couldn't.

Even though Bob was an outstanding pastor and teacher, the weakest area of his ministry was counseling. He found it difficult to be sympathetic to people who were hurting. He didn't have the patience to listen, and tended to address even the most serious problem with a simple verse and quick closing prayer. Deep down he often felt that his sobbing parishioners were weak. Why couldn't they simply trust God with their problems?

Then one day Bob's father died unexpectedly of an aneurysm. His dad was his best friend as well as his father. He was devastated. Suddenly Bob found himself facing the anguish of losing a loved one. His heart was broken and that brokenness changed his ministry dramatically.

Today, Bob is still an outstanding teacher, but ever since his father's death there has been a new depth to his messages and a new readiness to listen and cry with people in pain. Their tears now draw him close, as they once moved a compassionate Savior.

*Brokenness can become a bridge of compassion.*

> *Enlarge the place of your tent . . . lengthen your*
> *cords, and strengthen your stakes.*     —ISA. 54:2

Claire grinned every time she read this verse. She remembered reading it just before she found out she was pregnant with her first child. Wow, did God expand her life with that experience!

Blessing others? That thought really didn't cross her mind very often before she became a mom. Claire was thirty-one when she became a mother. She had been a hard-driven professional, consumed with her own self-interest.

Then something happened. It was an ordinary experience. Women give birth every day. But for Claire, becoming a mother changed her life dramatically. It enlarged her heart. As she opened her arms to her baby, she began to open her arms to other people. As she learned the joy of serving by becoming a parent, she began to serve others. Claire didn't really understand it herself, but she became more compassionate and open, a more giving person.

"I learned that the liberated life is not measured by how much of yourself you keep intact," she reflected, "but by how much you give away."

---

*Oh Lord, enlarge my heart.*

*The Spirit of the Lord will come upon you, and you will . . . be turned into another man.*
—1 SAM. 10:6

God uses the resources in our lives, who we are, and where we've been, to bless others. In addition, He gives us spiritual gifts. Spiritual gifts make us more than we are as natural individuals.

For example, you may find as you reach out to a hurting neighbor that something more than natural compassion is flowing through your warm hug. If people are blessed by your touch, it may be that God is developing in you the spiritual gift of healing.

Or as a co-worker feels free to share with you a sense of emptiness in her life, the Spirit may lead you to share your faith. He might give you a sensitivity to that person's need that surprises you, or words you've never before thought of. That is God blessing your human effort with supernatural power and, in the process, possibly birthing in you the gift of evangelism.

Spiritual gifts, like all gifts, need to be unwrapped, then used in order to bless others. As you learn about them and put them into practice, you will become more effective in God's service.

———————

*Lord, help me to discover what my spiritual gifts are and begin to grow in them.*

> *I chose you and appointed you that you should go*
> *and bear fruit, and that your fruit should remain.*
> —JOHN 15:16

The thought of job hunting these days is enough to fill anybody, even the confident and competent, with trepidation. We all know about the stiff competition. Every position draws swarms of applications; even the well-qualified are turned down. It's a matter of being in the right place at the right time, cultivating contacts, getting the inside edge, polishing your resumé, then waiting anxiously by the phone.

What a joy to know that God has a job waiting for you! He has chosen you. Your qualifications are just right. In fact, no one can do this job but you. As Lord of the universe, He has an incredible network. He knows the need; He knows the resources available to meet needs. And you are a resource: a wonderfully rich, talented, and gifted person, of incomprehensible worth.

As you discover what your special assignment is, you will not only be highly productive, but deeply fulfilled. And your work—raising children, sharing Christ with a friend, serving a neighbor—will have lasting value.

*Lord, thank You for gifting me. Show me how I can use my gifts for You today.*

*Blessed is the man whose strength is in You, whose heart is set on pilgrimage.*  —PS. 84:5

During the past month, we have been reflecting on how we can bless others, focusing on actions that bless; things we can do. Now we are going to turn our attention to a very special person, you, exploring who you *are*, not what you *do*.

You probably picked this book up because you wanted to learn how to bless your families and friends and those God calls you to love. As you've been reading, you've been challenged to think of new and creative ways to do that. But at the same time you may feel discouraged. Perhaps you feel too inadequate to be used by God to bless others.

Relax. Be kind to yourself. Becoming a person of blessing is a process, something we grow in day by day. Even as we long to affirm our children as we should, the old habit of scolding harshly may still slip out. A critical spirit may cause us to devalue, not build up our husbands. Will we ever learn?

Yes! Take joy in little successes, the constructive change you see, and move on in faith.

*Lord, help me to let go of the need to arrive, and rejoice in who I am, right now!*

*Continue in the things which you have learned and*
*been assured of.*
—2 TIM. 3:14

D o you remember all those sheets of tablet paper
your kindergartner brought home with rows and rows
of alphabet characters as he learned to write? Practice,
continuous practice, was the key to mastering the task.

Donna was asked to give a talk at church. She was
excited about it, but after the talk she felt sick inside.
She had such high expectations of herself and she
thought she'd failed. Disappointed in herself, she
walked off alone and wept.

The Lord seemed to be right beside her. "When
Tommy is discouraged because his drawing didn't
come out the way he wanted it to," said Jesus, "do you
refuse to give him anymore paper?"

Donna smiled. Her son was so hard on himself when
he made mistakes. She would always remind him that
there was a whole box of paper he could use, as much
as he wanted. Jesus said that's the way He felt about
her. He loved seeing her progress and would provide
whatever she needed to succeed.

With practice and God's help, Donna did succeed.
She became a very gifted speaker.

*Learning to bless others takes practice.*

*He lifted up His hands and blessed them. . . . While He blessed them, . . . He was parted from them and carried up into heaven.*

—LUKE 24:50–51

Jesus' last act on earth was to bless His disciples. He had journeyed with His disciples three years, intimately sharing his life with them. Walking side by side with Jesus, His friends had fallen into the rhythm of His vision and way of doing things.

But without Him? No one knew what would happen. Jesus knew their insecurity, their fears. He wanted to touch them and assure them they had learned what they needed to know—not everything, but enough to begin. And He would always be walking with them, sharing His heart through the Holy Spirit. They would remain connected.

As a lingering parent leaves a grieving child, Jesus reached out to touch His disciples before He ascended into heaven, to bless with His fingertips. But there was more than emotional comfort in that blessing. There was power.

In the Bible, blessing with the hands symbolized the transferring of power from one person to another. Jesus even promised them they would do even greater things than He.

*Lord, help me to remember that where my power to bless ends, Yours begins.*

*I am the vine, you are the branches. He who abides
in Me, and I in him, bears much fruit; for without
Me you can do nothing.*
                                    —JOHN 15:5

Before Jesus left the disciples, He summed up all that
He had taught into a few principles. Those principles
would empower them to lead the life of love He had
talked about. Those principles still offer helpful guide-
lines to anyone who wants to become a person of
blessing.

His first word was "stay connected." The disciples
had a clear choice: to remain connected to the life of
God, the Source of all blessing, and be fruitful, or to
try to manufacture that fruitfulness on their own and
produce nothing. Absolutely nothing—just as a
branch, disconnected from a tree is lifeless, dead, produces nothing.

We have the same choice. How do we stay connected so that that powerful life of blessing flows
through us? Jesus said to *abide* in Him. To abide, which
means to remain, to rest, to dwell in one place, sounds
like a foreign concept to modern ears. *Striving* we understand. But abiding? Have you ever heard the
branch of a tree grunting and groaning to produce
fruit? Not likely. The fruit comes in the fullness of time
as the sap, the life of the tree, feeds the branches. It's
a natural, relaxed process, and so our spiritual lives
should be.

---

*Lord, teach me to abide, not strive.*

*Pray without ceasing.*
—1 THESS. 5:17

Jesus stayed connected to the Father through prayer and so should we. Jesus' prayer life wasn't visible and showy like the public displays of the Pharisees. It was deep and hidden, and it was continuous. Jesus spent long hours in prayer, sometimes all night on a mountain alone, or in the pre-dawn hours. There were quiet moments with the disciples. And there were times when He looked up to the Father spontaneously to thank Him for what was in hand, such as when He blessed the five loaves and two fish that fed five thousand.

Prayer is the constant current of communication that flows between heaven and earth keeping Christians in close contact with God. The more frequently and fully that current flows, the more fruitful is the life of the believer.

Prayer is an expression of utter dependence on God as the source of all blessing. It can be the crying out of one in pain. It can be a cry of joy. It can be a sigh. It can be silence. It can be a dance of praise, rhythmical and fast, or it can be the stillness and quiet of a listening heart.

*Lord, draw me closer to You in prayer.*

*Let the beloved of the Lord rest secure in Him.*
—DEUT. 33:12 NIV

Dan was having his devotions early one morning. His wife, Kathy, came down the stairs and found him sitting at the dining room table, sound asleep, with his Bible open. Dan was startled when he saw Kathy. He felt guilty that he had fallen asleep.

"Don't," said Kathy. "You've just fallen asleep in the lap of the Lord."

Dan's eyes sparked up. "You're right. Why can't I just say, 'Daddy, I'm sleepy?'"

Prayer is simply being at home in God's presence, resting secure in His love for us. We cannot earn His love. It's a given. We cannot fail Him. His love for us is not based on a performance rating.

Sometimes in our prayer life, as in all of our endeavors, we try too hard. We feel guilty if we don't meet God every day in prayer. We chastise ourselves if our mind wanders while we are praying. If we are angry at God, we are afraid to let our feelings show.

The Father knows our feelings, our shortcomings, and loves us still. Let the heart of the Father welcome you and help you feel at ease.

---

*Prayer is a welcome place.*

*These things I have spoken to you, that My joy may
remain in you, and that your joy may be full.*
—JOHN 15:11

A person of blessing is a person of joy, deep joy. Joy
grounded in Jesus produces an inner radiance that attracts people.

For weeks, Kathleen had been trying to persuade
her neighbor to attend a Bible study at a nearby
church. Paula made excuses week after week; finally
she decided to go. She loved it and couldn't wait to go
back. What most drew her was not the teaching, but
the teacher, Kari Malcolm.

"Does Kari always smile like that?" Paula asked.

Kathleen assured Paula that she did. When Paula
learned about Kari's life, her joy seemed even more
amazing. The daughter of a missionary to China, Kari
had lost her father in a bombing raid during WWII.
When other teenagers were dreaming of dates and
parties, Kari was surviving as in a prisoner of war
camp.

Out of her suffering emerged a bold, infectious faith.
No one meeting Kari Malcolm could doubt where her
joy came from. Nor could they help but marvel at its
fullness.

_____

*Joy comes from Jesus, not our circumstances.*

> *Greater love has no one than this, than to lay down*
> *one's life for his friends.*            —JOHN 15:13

Jesus challenged His disciples, and He challenges us, to live a life of sacrifice. Jesus literally gave His life. In the Garden of Gethsemane we see Him wrestling with that terrible decision. In His agony, Scripture says, He sweat drops of blood.

Most of us will never be asked to make the ultimate sacrifice. But there are still times when each of us has to lay down something for others. It might be our pride as we ask forgiveness. It might be our agenda as we spend time with someone in need. It might be our fear as we ask for help for ourselves.

A person of blessing is a person in process—learning to be vulnerable, sensitive to the Spirit, shapable, yielding. We aren't so much called to be martyrs—to honor God with our physical death—but to honor Him by offering our bodies as living sacrifices, as Paul instructed the Romans (12:1). It is a dying to self.

It is by releasing self-will that God's will can be done. Without the Cross we wouldn't have redemption; without surrender, we wouldn't have great love.

---

*Saying no to our agenda frees us to say yes to God's.*

*Now I know that you fear God, since you have not withheld your son, your only son, from Me.*
—GEN. 22:12

As Diana had grown in Christ, she had yielded more and more of her life to God. But her career—that was different. Private, precious, exclusively hers. "Hands off," she told the Lord.

One Sunday she was sitting in a church service when the pastor said, "Whatever you do in life, whether you're a nurse, an executive, a postman, you need to share God's love with unbelievers."

That hit Diana hard. It had never occurred to her to use her writing career to share her faith. But that is what God led her to do.

God softened her stiff-necked stubbornness by giving her a baby daughter. Diana found herself ghost-writing a Christian parenting book, which to her surprise, she enjoyed a lot.

Several years later, Diana's mentor and best friend said, "I think you need to put your writing on the altar and be willing to sacrifice it for Christ." Diana was stunned. Give up writing altogether?

But Diana respected her friend's opinion. As she gave up what she loved, God poured out new talents—teaching, counseling, mentoring—that gave her even more joy.

*You can't outgive God.*

*Though I have all faith, so that I could remove*
*mountains, but have not love, I am nothing.*
—1 COR. 13:2

To become a person of blessing is to live a life of love. The well-known love chapter in 1 Corinthians describes what Christlike love looks like, manifested on a daily basis.

First, Paul says, to Christians who think they have arrived, even though you may have spiritual gifts like tongues, prophecy, faith, and giving, if you aren't loving, these amount to nothing.

Viv, a maturing Christian leader, reflected on this verse and felt convicted. She spent long hours in Bible study and volunteering at the church, but God seemed to say, "What about your brother?"

Viv's brother, a college freshman, was living with her and her husband while going to school. A typical 18-year-old, Luke wasn't much for helping around the house. Viv had grown resentful and bitter, but not until now did she see how her lack of love blocked communication with God and poisoned her other relationships. Not until she reconciled her relationship with her brother would love flow freely again.

---

*Is there lack of love in my life, Lord, toward another person?*

*Love suffers long and is kind.*
—1 COR. 13:4

A person of blessing is long-suffering, which means she is patient. Angela discovered this while watching her five-year-old learning to ride a bike. Angela was in the middle of something when Katie asked her for the umpteenth time to watch her ride her two-wheeler without training wheels.

Katie grinned from ear to ear as she wobbled ahead fifty feet instead of five, without help.

"That's great, honey," said Angela, feeling impatient and irritable. How long would this process take?

Suddenly Angela imagined Jesus standing beside her watching her daughter. The picture of patience and warm encouragement, He would be happy to see Katie enjoying herself in the now, not anxiously trying to push her ahead too fast into tomorrow. Katie would learn to ride her bike soon enough and this precious moment of learning would be gone forever.

Pride pushes and seeks to control. Humility stands back and allows things to happen. It values each person's individuality, allowing progress to come in a unique, authentic way.

*A controlling hand cannot bless.*

> *Love does not parade itself, is not puffed up.*
> —1 COR. 13:4

Sharon wanted to grow as a person of blessing, but felt that something was holding her back. She decided to ask the Lord in prayer what it might be.

A verse came to mind, "Behold, I stand at the door and knock" (Rev. 3:20). Sharon wondered, *Is there a room in my heart that I won't let Jesus enter?*

She saw Jesus enter a room called pride. The walls of the room were covered with trophies and plaques. It looked and felt cluttered. Jesus asked Sharon to take them down and make space for Him.

She did this and the room was swept clean. On the ledge where the trophies had been, Jesus put a simple, worn leather sandal, the kind He had worn. The sandal was meant to be a permanent fixture in this new room.

Sharon didn't realize how much pride had gotten in the way of what Jesus wanted to do. Letting it go released her to grow in giving.

*Is there a room in your life that you won't let Jesus enter?*

*[Love] does not behave rudely, does not seek its
own.*
                                          —1 COR. 13:5

Mom and Dad, please stop arguing," said Stacy, as
her parents began to raise their voices. She didn't
know what the argument was about, but it was getting
on her nerves.

The next day Stacy, a discerning six-year-old, said,
"Arguing is like one person trying to be taller than the
other. One person says 'I'm right.' " She put out two
hands, one on top of the other, to illustrate her point.
"Then the other person says, 'No, I'm right.' " She slid
the bottom hand out and put it on top of the upper
hand, then she put one hand on top of the other in fast
succession. "I'm right! I'm right! I'm right!"

Stacy's mom, who wanted to become a person of
blessing, suddenly realized what her daughter had
shown her. The reasons for the arguments must have
seemed childishly senseless to Stacy.

Stacy and her mother agreed that the only way to
de-escalate the anger was for one person to initiate
reconciliation. They put out their hands and shook.
"Let's be friends."

*A person of blessing is not self-seeking.*

> *Love never fails.*
> —1 COR. 13:8

For two years De had driven across town every week to help restore a couple's broken marriage. Tonight the peace-making panel had decided there was nothing more it could offer. As De watched the taillights of the couple's car disappear into the darkness, her heart was full of despair, not hope.

Pete and Carla were both from abusive homes. Carla was verbally abusive to Pete, and Pete had beaten Carla. They had turned to the Christian Conciliation Service, of which De was a part, as a last resort to see if they could resolve their conflicts before heading for the divorce courts.

De had poured out her heart to help, but it just didn't feel like it was enough. Three years later, De was thumbing through her phone book and called Carla, by mistake. After some small talk, De, hesitantly, asked how her marriage was going.

"Great!" Carla said. "You wouldn't believe it."

As De heard how much their relationship had improved and strengthened, she was stunned. Against all odds, love *had* prevailed.

---

*Lord, when I face impossible situations today, help me not to give up hope too soon.*

*When I was a child, I spoke as a child, I understood as a child. . . . but when I became a man, I put away childish things.*
                                   **—1 COR. 13:11**

Once a year Sally's church held a women's retreat. As a new church member, Sally thought this would be a great opportunity to make friends. The first night at the dinner table, she joined in the conversation, acting interested in what everyone had to say, but she felt a distance. When someone made a comment, she thought, *How trivial!* or *I can't believe someone would think that way.*

Sally was ashamed of her attitude. She wanted to be accepting toward everyone, but that old critical attitude often got in the way. She understood the root of her problem: it was her "new-kid-on-the-block" insecurity. As a child, she had moved a lot and always felt she didn't fit into a new neighborhood or school. She protected herself, as an outsider, by feeling arrogant and self-righteous, thinking, *I'm better than you.* As an adult, whenever she found herself in a new social setting, she reverted to that old behavior.

Becoming a person of blessing for Sally meant "putting away" that childish behavior by naming it, confessing it, and asking Christ to give her His mind and heart for people.

*Lord, thank You that in You I'm a "new creation," ever-changing, ever-growing.*

*For now we see in a mirror, dimly, but then face to face. Now I know in part, but then I shall know just as I also am known.* — 1 COR. 13:12

A person of blessing gradually begins to see herself as she really is, deeply and fully loved by Jesus.

Our self-image is formed by the way we see ourselves. That image is rarely a true picture. It is so often clouded with hurt, disappointments, unmet expectations. Add to that the hurt and disappointments that other people project onto us, and the picture becomes even more distorted.

The mark of maturity for a Christian is to ground one's self-image in Jesus, to learn to see Him face to face in prayer, in Scripture, in worship. Something mysterious and wonderful happens as we do that. We are transformed.

"Only as I receive God's love in my spirit," writes Margaret Therkelsen, "can I become the person he created me to be . . . I feel valuable and worthwhile. My sense of self-esteem, built on his esteem for me, develops as his love reveals how precious I am."[4]

Seeing ourselves as truly valuable and worthwhile releases us to be our best.

*Lord, thank You for the depth of Your love for me. Help me to see it more clearly day by day.*

*Blessed are the pure in heart, for they shall see God.*
—MATT. 5:8

It is by coming into the presence of God that a person of blessing draws strength to bless others. We exalt Him, worship Him, love Him; then, drawing close to His holiness, confess any sin that might block fellowship with Him. For most of us, confession isn't very thorough.

One mother learned the reality of this when she saw how her seven-year-old cleaned her bedroom. Meghan wanted to go to the park. They would go, Mom said, as soon as her room was clean. Meghan dashed upstairs and returned in five minutes. "Come and see, Mom," she said beaming. "It's white as snow!"

Meghan's room did look spotless. It was only when her mom opened the closet door that Meghan's stashed-away-out-of-sight piles were discovered. That's what we try to do with God, this mom reflected; we stash our sins away and appear to have a cleaned-up life.

David prayed wisely, "Wash me thoroughly from my iniquity" (Ps. 51:2). The cleaner our hearts are, the more clearly we can see God.

*Lord, show me any unacknowledged sin in my heart; cleanse me deeply and completely.*

> *Let the words of my mouth and the meditation of*
> *my heart be acceptable in Your sight, O LORD.*
> —PS 19:14

Blessing springs forth from our hearts: our thought life, our deepest feelings. We cannot be a source of blessing if our attitudes are unpleasing to God.

For example, the prophet Isaiah warns that judgmentalism (putting other people down in our thoughts) can be oppressive. It creates an invisible burden that someone has to bear. Likewise, unconfessed sin, hidden in the heart of the one pointing the finger, blocks blessing to that one too.

If we think of God's blessing as a free-flowing river, then we can see that judgmentalism, hard and unmoving, acts like a dam to stop the generous outpouring of our heavenly Father's love.

So we hear the Father pleading that we would do away with our critical spirits and "be like a watered garden, and like a spring of water whose waters do not fail" (Isa. 58:11).

"Accept others as I accept you; forgive as I forgive. And see what happens!" we might hear Him say. "Your life will be saturated with My love and bring forth an abundance of good things. You will become a channel of blessing, bringing refreshment to others."

*Am I letting God's love flow freely through me?*

*Blessed are the people who know the joyful sound!*
*They walk, O LORD, in the light of*
*Your countenance.*

—PS. 89:15

A person of blessing is in perpetual awe of God's goodness. When you awoke this morning, you woke to a world lit with God's love.

God pours out His blessings to us every day, but we are so preoccupied we may miss His overtures. Dashing here and there, we give the world a quick glance, rarely taking time to drink in the beauty of God's good creation, to receive its blessing and His blessing.

God is the giver of good gifts. To receive God's gifts, sometimes we need to let go of crowded schedules and all the distractions that clamor for our attention.

God has given you this day to enjoy. Instead of dashing out the door this morning, take a moment to look outside your window. Let your eye rest on something lovely, focus on the near-at-hand. In prayer, open your heart to let God bless you through the beauty you see.

*Lord, let my day be filled with little glimpses of You.*

> *The LORD is . . . loving toward all he
> has made.* —PS. 145:13 NIV

Mister, are you God?" asked a little boy in rags as he held a sack full of freshly baked chocolate donuts in his hands. The young boy was one of many orphans roaming the streets of London during World War II. And the man who bent down and gently put the bag in his hands was General Dwight Eisenhower.

The general had decided to walk the few blocks to his headquarters that day instead of taking a staff car. As he walked past a bakery, the delicious smell of fresh bread and pastries floated through the air. That was when he noticed two boys with their noses pressed up against the bakery windows, looking longingly at the donuts.

Ike's staff looked on skeptically as he asked his orderly to buy the donuts, which he gave to the boys. It was a small act of kindness, but an act so full of tenderness and love that the children thought it must be God Himself who had stooped down to answer their need.

When a person of blessing moves with the impulses of God's love, acts of loving-kindness, no matter how insignificant, have a startling impact.

---

*Lord, help me to be attentive today to little acts of kindness that show others how much You value them.*

*In quietness and confidence shall be
your strength.*      —ISA. 30:15

It is easy, as a source of blessing, to become depleted, always giving out to others. At those times of emptiness, we need to fill ourselves again with God's love to renew our strength.

One way to do this is to rest in silence. We are so caught up in a whirlwind of activity, we forget that all of creation is not rushing at the same frantic pace. Take a look out your window. Look at the trees. Not a bough sways, not a leaf rustles. All is peaceful in the woods. Breathtaking. Look at the sky, vast, immeasurable, revealing the great expanse of God's faithfulness.

"In Him," says Paul, "we live and move and have our being" (Acts 17:28). It is good, at times, to feel hidden in His heart and to just rest there.

"Is not the LORD your God with you? And has He not given you rest on every side?" asked David (1 Chron. 22:18).

If God has given us rest, shouldn't we accept that gift as a blessing and let it nourish our bodies and our souls?

*Lord, may I enter Your rest.*

*Teach me Your way, O Lᴏʀᴅ; I will walk in Your
truth; unite my heart. . . .*                    —PS 86:11

Sometimes we don't feel God's wholeness because we
are fragmented. If we are at war with ourselves, both
sides lose.

Connie was struggling with two sides of her personality: the "Martha" side and the "Mary" side, the demanding, scurrying, get-things-done side and the
unhurried, contemplative side that loved to sit still and
listen to Jesus.

At times, Connie pictured herself running away into
a locked room to pray where she could be safe from
Martha's tyranny. One day she realized she could not
escape or deny the Martha part of her personality.

Martha and Mary needed to become friends. So
Mary left her room of prayer and put loving arms
around Martha. Connie couldn't be Mary all the time;
she needed to be a doer, not just a thinker. And there
were times when poor Martha needed to rest, put up
her feet, and have her inner batteries charged.

*I will be kind to myself and accepting. Only as a whole person can
I find balance and energy to bless others.*

*Finally, my brethren, be strong in the Lord and in the power of His might. Put on the whole armor of God, that you may be able to stand against the wiles of devil.*
—EPH. 6:10–11

In becoming a person of blessing, we must take authority over battles inside our own hearts that deplete our energy. We also need to be aware that our desire to bless, which comes from God, will meet spiritual resistance.

Have you ever tried to be a peacemaker, and had your shins kicked? Have you ever tried to affirm someone and been attacked by a host of self-condemning thoughts that remind you of what a terrible person *you* are?

Where does that resistance come from? Jesus said that He came to give us a full life in all its abundance. Satan's avowed purpose, on the other hand, is to steal, kill, and destroy. In this eternal battle of light and darkness, blessing and cursing, a mature Christian needs to recognize that there is warfare and learn to defend herself.

That we might defend ourselves against the spiritual forces of evil, God has given us armor for our protection and to help us move out with confidence in His might. Putting on the armor listed in Ephesians 6:14–17 will strengthen your power to bless.

*Blessing others can be a battle. Lord, teach me to arm myself with Your strength.*

> *Therefore it shall be, when you have crossed over*
> *the Jordan. . . . you shall build an altar to the*
> LORD.
>
> —DEUT. 27:4–5

A person of blessing knows the value of praise and thanksgiving—not only to enthrone God in our thoughts, but also to keep our focus fixed on Him.

Cheryl was worried. There was talk of lay-offs at work. Bruce had just started with a new company. No one knew how well it would fare in an uncertain economic climate. Summer was coming and the children were signed up for camps and athletics. She dreaded the thought of having to tell them one more time that they'd have to make sacrifices.

Unemployment was the thing Cheryl feared the most. They had been through it so many times before, just the thought of unemployment filled her with anxiety.

In the midst of this, the Lord seemed to say "build an altar." After the Israelites had crossed the Jordan into the promised land, God told them to build an altar as a reminder of God's faithfulness.

So she did. Cheryl began to recall how God had carried them through so much. Always He had provided. Celebrating those answers to prayer strengthened her faith for the future.

---

*A person of blessing looks back with gratitude.*

*Go therefore and make disciples . . .*
—MATT. 28:19

How does one continue to grow as a person of blessing? There are no schools that offer courses on the subject, no university degrees. Jesus taught by example. The disciples learned to emulate His life-style by constant companionship, rubbing shoulders with Him, sharing His life on a daily basis. He told His disciples to do the same.

You can listen to sermons on the life of love, read books and watch videos, but the surest way to learn how to bless others is to be in close companionship with someone else who does it well.

"Your drive to learn, explore, and become more Christlike has encouraged me to do the same," wrote a friend who had been discipled by another. "Thanks for your friendship and encouragement."

We all follow our own paths of growth. But there are times when it's helpful to walk alongside another who perhaps has walked ahead. A mentor doesn't have to be an expert or renowned authority on the spiritual life. She can be someone very close at hand, a young mom like you, a friend at Bible study, or an older woman in your church whose heart for service you admire.

*On the road to growth, it's good to have a partner.*

> *Every good gift and every perfect gift is from above.*
>
> —JAMES 1:17

A person of blessing looks at each day as a gift from God. "I just take one day," says Mother Teresa. "Yesterday is gone. Tomorrow has not come. We have only today to love Jesus."

What can happen in just one day? Can you turn around an unhealthy relationship by suddenly expressing high value to a husband you've devalued all your married life? Can words of affirmation immediately soften the heart of a child who has become accustomed to the harsh tones of an angry parent?

What can happen in just one day? Eleanor had prayed for decades that her mother would come to know Christ. It hurt her so much to see this special woman living apart from God's blessing. As her mom lay dying of cancer, Eleanor's mother finally asked Eleanor how she could find the joy her daughter had found. Eleanor prayed with her mother who, that day, accepted Jesus as her Savior.

"All my life I have been going in one direction," said her mother. "Today I know I am walking in another." Five days later, Eleanor's mother was with the Lord.

*A journey of a thousand miles begins with a single step.*

*And he called the twelve to Him, and began to send them out two by two.*        —MARK 6:7

Jesus sent out His disciples two by two so they could offer each other mutual companionship, support, and encouragement.

A disciple is a learner. Jesus' discipleship method of one person learning from another is a wonderful way to become more effective in blessing others. At the same time you are learning from someone else, you can be sharing with another what you've learned.

We equip others to bless by example. One mom picks up a creative idea for blessing her children from another mom. A young wife is encouraged by an older woman who has weathered the storms of those first stressful years of marriage.

In the best discipling friendships, both friends learn from one another. With different gifts, talents, and strengths, each may be in different places in various growth areas.

In the next few days, we'll look at how elements of the blessing can be used to equip others to bless.

*Lord, thank You for friends who have encouraged me and for friends I can encourage.*

*A woman came having an alabaster flask of very costly oil of spikenard. And she broke the flask and poured it on His head.*
—MARK 14:3

When Regina and Sissy volunteered to put together several slide shows for a church retreat, they had no idea what they'd be getting into. The shows took long hours to prepare. On the day of the retreat, they were exhausted, but pleased that the slide shows went smoothly.

After the retreat, Darlene, the retreat leader, came up to Regina and Sissy. No one else had any idea how much work the shows had been, but Darlene knew. She expressed her appreciation for their sacrifice of time. Then she did something that Regina would never forget.

Darlene put her arms around both women and prayed, very intimately, very tenderly: "Lord, these women, like the woman who poured costly perfume on Your head, have poured out their time and energy in a beautiful gesture of love. Bless them for what they've given."

Through Darlene's affirmation of touch and words, Regina felt loved and highly valued. It was as if perfume had been poured over her! Inspired by Darlene, Regina would one day lead her own retreats to share God's blessing with others.

---

*Pouring out our best for others inspires them to do the same.*

*And I was afraid, and went and hid your talent in
the ground.*                              —MATT. 25:25

God gives us gifts and talents to use, but often we
undervalue who we are and don't have the courage to
step out and use them. An affirming friend can make
the difference between someone who buries her talents in the ground and one who releases her talents to
bless others.

Consider this letter of thanks from someone who
yearns to be used by God and is just discovering how
worthy and gifted she is. "I feel like such an infant in
my walk with God, but my legs are strong and my
heart is full. I am hope-filled," she writes an encouraging friend. "I've felt awkward asking for God to bless
me because I feel so unworthy. Your message, for some
reason, has given me the OK to ask. Please pray for
me. I want so much to serve Him."

This woman already has the greatest gift of all: a
desire to serve others. All that she needs to translate
that desire into concrete action is the permission to believe in herself. How empowering an affirming word
can be to a woman like this!

*Lord, teach me to recognize and affirm gifts in others so they can
serve You.*

*December 2* – DEVELOPING GIFTS

> *Well done, good and faithful servant; you have
> been faithful over a few things, I will make you
> ruler over many things.* —MATT. 25:23

Picturing a special future for someone who wants to
grow as a person of blessing involves challenging her
to realize her full potential. Just like an employer who
gives us more responsibility when he feels we are
ready to take it on, God gradually gives us more challenging assignments to develop our gifts.

Gwen met with hurting women to offer counsel and
prayer. Tina was Gwen's prayer partner. Tina did not
want to be on the front lines of such a ministry, but she
was a faithful prayer partner for Gwen. As Tina prayed
with and for Gwen, she too developed a heart for hurting women.

Gwen was not surprised when she got a note from
Tina some years later telling her about a woman who
had shared some deep heart hurts with her. "I remember you warned us," wrote Tina, "that if we truly
sought to love and help others, people would turn up.
How right you are!"

Tina was on her way to taking on bigger assignments.

———————

*So many are hungry for Your blessing, Lord. Help me not to hold
back when You give me a greater opportunity to bless others.*

*And they said to one another, "Did not our heart
burn within us while He talked with us on the road,
and while He opened the Scriptures to us?"*
—LUKE 24:32

One of the pitfalls of discipleship is that an eager disciple can become too dependent, preventing rather than promoting her own growth.

Such was the case with Bobby and her mentor-friend, Margaret. There was so much that Bobby wanted to know and Margaret, who knew the Bible well, seemed to have all the answers.

When the time came for Margaret to move away, Bobby felt a sense of panic. Then, in prayer one day, Bobby saw a picture of herself walking along a path, enjoying Margaret's company when Jesus came alongside them. Margaret, with a smile, handed Bobby's hand to Jesus, then she left. Jesus said, "Through the years, Margaret will come and go. But I will be here, always."

Bobby began to realize that she had wanted Margaret to give her all the answers without doing any of the work herself. Jesus promised that He would open the Scriptures for her as He had done for Margaret. And He did. When Bobby met Margaret again, she had insights of her own to share.

*Lord, help me to remember there are three on the road: me, my friend, and You.*

*A disciple is not above his teacher, but everyone who is perfectly trained will be like his teacher.*
—LUKE 6:40

There are seasons of change in a mentoring relationship just as there are in any friendship. The only way to maintain active commitment is to be honest with one another as both members change and grow.

Jane had mentored Emily for fifteen years. During that time, Emily went from an adoring disciple to a mature leader on her own. They both felt it was time to share their feelings about the changing nature of their relationship.

"A mentor position can feel more spiritual than it is," Jane reflected in a letter. "But a peer position has to face the good things God gives friends like you. A peer position requires patience and humility as He uses His lovely grace poured out in you to show me areas in which I need to change."

The relationship had shifted and Jane was now learning from Emily. Emily admitted that as she had outgrown the need for a mentor, she felt a greater need for Jane to be a friend.

Both women agreed that they saw each other more completely now. And no matter how much they could teach each other, they would always be students of the one great Teacher they both admired.

---

*While journeying with another, it is good to share your feelings frequently.*

*Whoever heeds correction gains understanding.*
—PROV. 15:32 NIV

Besides one-on-one encouragement from a friend, another way to grow more effective in blessing others is to surround yourself with a small group of friends with whom you meet on a regular basis for mutual support and accountability.

During the early years of my (John's) marriage, I met with five men who challenged me to grow as a husband and a father by lovingly holding me accountable for my actions. One man actually called my wife each week to check up on my progress. I was also free to do spot-checks on his family.

Small-group settings allow us to be honest about the temptations and struggles we all face. Often those outside our family circle can see problems we are not aware of and be able to share valuable insights for resolutions from their own experience.

Only the wise seek correction, says Scripture. What are you doing to build love and support in your home? Questions like that, asked by a caring group of people who love and support us, can hold us to our goals and spur us on to greater growth.

*You can't make it alone. You don't have to.*

> *Imitate me, just as I also imitate Christ.*
> —1 COR. 11:1

As parents, the closest disciples committed to our care are our children. Watching us model Christ in our daily lives is the best way for our children to catch a vision of Christ and become people of blessing.

Even though Ray grew up in a Christian home, he didn't become a Christian until he was an adult. As a new believer, Ray was troubled by the image of a Christian as weak in contrast to the macho image he had been taught to aspire to. "How can I be a Christian and still be a man?" he asked God.

The heavenly Father brought to Ray's mind a picture of his dad's face. His father lived thousands of miles away, and Ray hadn't seen him for years. Remembering his dad's face now, he noticed how kind his father's eyes were, something he had never thought about before. God seemed to be saying, "Be like your father." Ray knew that his dad was highly respected by other men for his kind firmness. "God had provided a human model, one He placed right in front of my eyes," said Ray.

---

*Lord, help me to walk in Your footsteps as my children walk in mine.*

*Every eye will see Him.*
—REV. 1:7

Do your children see Jesus in your eyes? One little boy did.

"Mom, do you ever see God behind people's eyeballs?" asked Amy's five-year-old.

"What do you mean?"

"You know. You look at them and you see Jesus in there."

"No," Amy confessed. "Do you?"

"Yes," said her son. "I see Him in you."

A modest mother, Amy tells this story with not the slightest hint of pride. She was floored when Cory paid her that incredible compliment. Of course, she talked to him about Jesus in daily conversation and she hoped her actions reflected the love of the Lord, but Cory's comment made her realize that she communicated Jesus to her son not only in words and actions, but also in who she was.

Children see with greater clarity than we sometimes give them credit for. More than saying and doing all the right things—surface actions—it is the depth of our personal relationship with Jesus Christ that will help our sons and daughters catch the vision of who Jesus is.

*Oh, Lord, give me a burning faith that can radiate Your love to my children.*

> *Oh, taste and see that the LORD is good.*
> —PS. 34:8

God is the Source of blessing, the One from whom all blessing flows. The first step in equipping our children to bless is to lead them to the Source of blessing.

As a child, Judy loved to dance down the stairs in the morning and head for the kitchen just as her mother was taking fresh bread from the oven. Just remembering that lovely aroma made her mouth water. Now as a mother, she wished that her daughter could share the same experience. But her mother had never taught her to bake bread so she couldn't pass it on to Crystal. Why hadn't she taught her?

"There were four children in the family," says Judy. "Mom got up at five in the morning when she had some peace and quiet to get the job done. She probably didn't involve us because it was too much trouble."

Faith-building, like bread-baking, is a process. If we just serve up our children the finished product of our faith experience, not including them in the process, how can they ever find a faith that is their own? Only by tasting and seeing that God is good themselves will faith become theirs.

---

*What can I do today to help my children taste God's goodness?*

*Behold, I stand at the door and knock. If anyone*
*hears My voice and opens the door, I will come in.*
—REV. 3:20

In teaching children, a picture really is worth a thousand words. Most Sunday school teachers use this verse in Revelation to ask children the question, "Do you want to ask Jesus into your heart?"

One mother decided to picture this concept for her children by drawing a large door on a piece of paper and taping it to the inside of their bedroom doors as a vivid reminder of Jesus' gracious invitation. One by one, they did open their heart doors to Christ.

In the Bible, Jesus is pictured as a warm friend to children. Little ones readily respond to the picture of Jesus as a shepherd, carrying a little lamb on His shoulders. One mother taped that picture on the bedpost of her little one's bed so that he would be reminded of Jesus' constant presence carrying him through the night.

Another mom gave her daughter a picture of Jesus cupping His hands around the face of a little girl, smiling tenderly at her. *That's how Jesus looks at me*, the daughter thought. What a gift that picture of affection was, a gift she could treasure for life.

*What a friend my children have in Jesus.*

*And whoever gives one of these little ones only a
cup of cold water in the name of a disciple, . . . he
shall by no means lose his reward.*

—MATT. 10:42

God promises to reward our smallest efforts when we
disciple little ones.

Jane was exhausted after her first week of teaching
Sunday school. She wondered how she was going to
make it through the year, but she did make it. Every
week, she stretched her mind to come up with a creative way to make abstract concepts real. To illustrate
the verse, "Cast your cares on Him because He cares
for you," she filled a basket with rocks and had each
child take one out. They could feel how much lighter
the basket became with the removal of each rock.

On her last day of teaching, Jane talked about God's
love. She said that everyone has an empty space in
their heart for God to fill. She poured water into a glass
as she said this. As God fills our hearts with His love,
it spills out to others. She poured water from the first
glass into others. As she did this, the Sunday school
supervisor came to thank Jane for her work. She gave
her a small gift along with today's verse about giving
little ones a cup of water.

Coincidence? Jane didn't think so. It clearly illustrated to her how much God valued her teaching.

*Teaching little ones is no small thing.*

*And you shall love the LORD your God with all your heart, with all your soul, with all your mind, and with all your strength.*
—MARK 12:30

If God has top priority in our lives, sometimes we are disappointed when our children don't share our same degree of commitment. However, we may find that with more commitment to our children, we may be able to raise their sense of value of God.

Grant's junior high son began to skip Sunday school nine times out of ten. Grant asked his son, on a scale of one to ten, where did God rate? The boy answered honestly: God rated about sixth place—right after television.

Instead of getting angry, Grant patiently asked his son what it would take to move God to a higher place of value in his life.

His son confided that the real problem with Sunday school was that he felt embarrassed because he didn't know the Bible verses and where to find them when his teacher called on him.

Grant decided to meet with his son weekly and go over the junior high lessons. After several months of studying the Bible together, Grant's son was regularly attending his class, and studying God's Word together actually drew father and son closer than they'd ever been before.

———

*Lord, show me how I can help my children make You a top priority in their lives.*

*It is written, "My house shall be called a house of prayer."*
                                        —MATT. 21:13

Whenever something was lost in the Johnson household, everyone was prone to fall apart. To stop the wails and tears, Mom advised, "Let's stop and pray about it." It only took a few moments to do that, and invariably they found what they were looking for.

There were times, however, when Mrs. Johnson forgot her own advice. When she became frazzled looking for something, her children would remind her, "Have you stopped and prayed about it?"

Our homes should be houses of prayer—places where our children learn the importance of being grounded in Jesus every minute of the day, where they discover how to draw on the Source of Blessing to meet their needs and the needs of others.

As soon as our children learn these things at home, they naturally begin to reach out to others. Jenny, a first grader in the Johnson family, came home one day and told her mother about a friend at school who had been crying. Jenny had taken her into the cloak room and prayed about the problem. "It made her feel a lot better, Mom," said Jenny, who was already becoming a person of blessing.

---

*Lord, help me to make my home a house of prayer.*

*I have fought the good fight, . . . I have kept the
faith.*
—2 TIM. 4:7

When Maren was four, her mother used to wonder
what she was doing when she would march around the
outer edges of their front yard. Maren would walk
right along the sidewalk as far from the house as she
could. With her brow furrowed and eyes downcast, she
looked deep in thought.

When Maren explained what was going on inside of
her, she gave a graphic description of the battle of
darkness and light that wages in all of us.

"When I do something wrong," she said, "I can see
a black cloud in my mind. It comes between me and
Jesus and I can't see Him anymore. Then when I say
I'm sorry, the cloud goes away."

Maren understood that sin separates us from God
and each other. When she was feeling alienated from
those she loved, she literally separated herself. Her
march around the yard was a prayer march, a time of
wrestling with making a difficult decision to confess a
wrong or to forgive someone. She knew what to do,
but it was hard to do it. Every time she won a battle,
she stood a little firmer in her faith.

*Lord, strengthen my children as they strive to stand firm in their faith.*

> *You who make your boast in the law, do you*
> *dishonor God through breaking the law?*
> —ROM. 2:23

Jamie was a nine-year-old who was swayed by her friends not to invite her cousin to her slumber party. "She's too fat and ugly!" they jeered.

Jamie's mom learned later that her niece was deeply hurt by being excluded. Jamie's mom wanted to show Jamie the difference between honoring and dishonoring actions in a memorable way.

One night when Jamie was taking a bath, her mom asked her how much the steam weighed that was coming up from the tub. "Not very much," Jamie said.

Then her mom handed her Dad's paperweight and asked her how much that weighed.

"Tons!"

"When you dishonor people," her mom explained, "you treat them lightly as if they are not worth much, but when you honor them, you treat them as if they are important and carry a lot of weight.

"When you excluded your cousin, you treated her as if she wasn't worth much and your action also dishonored God."

With tears in her eyes, Jamie prayed and asked God to forgive her, then hardest of all, she called her cousin and apologized. _____

*As You honor them, Lord, help my children to learn to honor others.*

*And whoever exalts himself will be abased, and he who humbles himself will be exalted.*
—MATT. 23:12

Be gracious, Carrie, if you run into any Almond Joys today," Larry winked at his wife.

Carrie's team, the Chicklets, had just won the city soccer championship and, as a third grader, Carrie would be tempted to gloat if she ran into one of her opponents at school.

As a wise father, Larry treated his admonition in a light-hearted manner, but it was a serious reminder. Humility is not seen as a virtue in a performance-oriented culture like ours. It will never be a value that is easily caught by those around us; it must be consciously taught by Christians who aim to model Jesus.

As parents, we tend to think of all the good lessons we can teach our children if they fail. But it can be just as difficult for children (adults too!) to handle winning and losing.

Being on top of the pack provides a ready temptation to put down others, to devalue, instead of honor. Even in those circumstances—*particularly* in those circumstances—we are called to bless and affirm others through our actions and words.

*Lord, help me to equip my children for success as well as failure.*

> *"Lord, how often shall my brother sin against me,*
> *and I forgive him? Up to seven times?"* . . . *"Up to*
> *seven times seven,"* [*answered Jesus*].
> —MATT. 18:21–22

One of the most important ways our children can express high value to others is to forgive. Opportunities to learn this occur throughout each day.

Brenna, a five-year-old, was trying to read a book to her little sister, Carey. Carey hit Brenna and yanked the book away.

"Carey!" Brenna screamed and ran to her bedroom.

Afterwards, her mom came to her room to talk. "Mom," Brenna asked, "why did she do that? I was just trying to help."

Her mother sympathized with her older daughter, but she needed to understand that she had to be compassionate toward her younger sister. She hugged her and said, "Jesus forgives us, honey, because He knows we are weak. We need to forgive in the same way. Carey's just a baby. She doesn't know better."

"I was so mad at her," Brenna said, gritting her teeth, "I wanted to kill her."

It wasn't easy to forgive that day. It would never be easy, but it would always be right.

---

*To err is human, to forgive divine.*

*But if you do not forgive men their trespasses,*
*neither will your Father forgive your trespasses.*
                                    —MATT. 6:15

Unforgiveness blocks blessing from the Father, which is why it is so important not to sweep hurt under the rug. But forgiveness can't be forced. It has to be genuine, "from the heart," as Scripture says.

"Don't ever do what my father did," said Shari's dad. "He would sit me on a chair and tell me I could go out and play when I said I was sorry. That made me feign repentance. I was dishonest with my dad and dishonest with myself."

Shari took that as a wise word of caution. It made her think of ways to help her children express their feelings honestly.

Sometimes her children found it easier to draw pictures of their feelings or to write a note instead of saying the words. That was fine. "I'm sorry for what I did, Mom," wrote one daughter. "Please forgive me! I love you and didn't mean to hurt your feelings. Love, your best friend." One tender note simply read, "I'm sorry. I feel like crying." It was illustrated with a frowning face dropping big teardrops.

*Forgiveness is a process that has to be gently worked through.*

> *I have set before you life and death, blessing and cursing; therefore choose life.* —DEUT. 30:19

Children can be taught that they have a choice to bless or curse by their actions and words.

Herbie and AJ were next-door neighbors and best friends. Sandra, Herbie's mom, had taken them to a park event. It was a fun outing, but they came home fighting.

"You pushed in front of me!"

"I did not!"

"Did too!"

Exasperated, Sandra said, "Boys, you are good friends. But when you get together you always end up fighting. Why?"

"Well, it's your fault," one pointed a finger.

"It's *your* fault," said the other.

They were an an impasse. Then a thought occurred to Sandra: switch tracks.

"Did anything fun happen tonight?" she asked the boys. "Try to remember one good thing."

Immediately, the mood changed. Herbie smiled. "Remember the time you pushed me down the hill, AJ, and we both rolled down together?"

They laughed. Their minds were alive now with happy memories. "Remember when . . ."

---

*Lord, help me to teach my children to accentuate the positive.*

> [*God comforts us*] *that we may be able to comfort*
> *those who are in any trouble, with the comfort with*
> *which we ourselves are comforted by God.*
> —2 COR. 1:4

Children can learn very easily to bless others through touch. As Mom holds them to kiss away an "owie," they find it natural to lay a loving hand on someone who is hurting.

Kate often laid her hand on her daughter's forehead to pray for a fever to subside. Even as the sickness was waning, Jennifer would ask her mom to pray for her because she enjoyed the nurturing, as well as the healing touch of her mother's hand.

One night at the dinner table, the family was praying for Dad's bad back. Instead of just praying in words, Jennifer got up and put her arms around her Dad as she prayed for Jesus to heal the pain there. She had learned from her mother that touch can be a channel for God's healing. Unexpected tears ran down her father's cheeks at his daughter's expression of love.

Another mom, a single mother, missing the physical affection of a husband, felt loved and cared for when her boys would give her a hug. "They just seem to know when I am feeling low and need the touch of encouragement."

*What a source of blessing little ones' comfort can be!*

*Therefore encourage each other with these words.*
—1 THESS. 4:18 NIV

Children's words, so tender and sincere, can be a wonderful way to bless family and friends.

June was having a hard week. Everything that could go wrong did. She had gotten a speeding ticket, forgotten to take the cat to the vet, burned a casserole, and to top it all off, Saturday was her fortieth birthday. How depressing!

Imagine how surprised she was when she found a plate of cookies and milk beside her bed with a note from her nine-year-old. "I thought I would do a little treat for you just for being our mom. Love, Winnie." It felt wonderful to be loved just for "being her," despite her mistakes. With those few affirming words from her daughter, her week turned around completely.

A few scribbled words of thanks or appreciation sent to a relative or a crayoned picture of a teddy bear with a short message to cheer up a sick friend can be a great source of encouragement—especially to people who don't have children in their daily lives.

*I will encourage my children to share their blessing words with others.*

*Though the mountains be shaken and the hills be removed, yet my unfailing love for you will not be shaken.*
—ISA. 54:10 NIV

As our children become people of blessing, sometimes we are the ones who receive the greatest rewards.

Lisa's face burst into tears. She had left her teddy bear behind in the store where she and her mother had just been shopping. They went back and looked, but it couldn't be found. Linda was perturbed. "I told you to leave it at home. You'll just have to learn the hard way."

That night, as Linda was taking out her contacts, she dropped one down the sink. "Oh, no, Lisa, what am I going to do? Mommy made a dumb mistake."

Lisa looked sympathetically at Linda and said, "I know how you feel, Mom." Lisa gave her mom a big hug.

Linda couldn't believe how tender and caring her daughter could be after she had been so harsh to her. Lisa prayed for the contact to be found, and it was.

"Dear Jesus," Lisa prayed at bedtime that night, "thank You so much for helping my mommy and me. We just have to learn the hard way. Those things were important to us, especially Mommy's contact." Linda was touched by her daughter's unfailing love.

*Thank You, Father, for the blessings our children pour out on us.*

> *Even a child is known by his deeds.*
> —PROV. 20:11

We should encourage our children to bless those beyond their familiar circle of family and friends.

Billy was a child at church who had diabetes. As his diabetes worsened, he was confined to a wheelchair and then went blind. Coleen and her six-year-old daughter, Kelsi, visited Billy once a month. They were stunned to find out one day that Billy's bedroom was destroyed by fire. He was OK, but he lost all of his belongings.

Coleen and Kelsi were praying for Billy to find a new house, when Kelsi started wondering what it would be like to have your bedroom destroyed by fire. "That means all his clothes are gone. And his pajamas. And his Bible was burned up."

Kelsi's eyes lit up. Kelsi didn't want to just pray for Billy. She wanted to *do* something. "I know. I could send him my little Bible with a letter. If he doesn't have his Bible, what will he do when he does something wrong?" So Kelsi sent Billy her pocket-sized Bible and he treasured it even though he couldn't read it. It comforted him just to know that a little girl was holding him close in her prayers.

*Lord, may my children be equipped to bless with actions as well as words.*

*Inasmuch as you did it to one of the least of these*
*My brethren, you did it to Me.*      —MATT. 25:40

Teaching our children to bless others, especially those in need, teaches them to express high value to all men and women. Jesus says it also expresses high value to Him.

Children can be taught the habit of giving at an early age. Little hands can help fill a grocery bag with canned goods for a local hunger drive. Taking our children to visit food banks and to participate in feeding programs in the inner city can sensitize them to the needs of others and provide ways they can serve.

Pennies collected in an offering bank can add up quickly to make a sizable contribution, especially when distributed in the Third World where pennies can buy more. Nine-year-old Whitney proudly told her parents that she was going to give five dollars of her allowance to a World Vision hunger project. *Her* five dollars would be used to re-seed a farmer's field in Kenya that could feed a whole family.

These opportunities not only provide a way for children to act out their faith tangibly, but they also make them feel their contributions count.

*Blessing others also helps our children value themselves more highly.*

*Freely you have received, freely give.*
—MATT. 10:8

Christmas was coming, and Bev wanted her children to think about giving instead of receiving. There were always projects to get involved in, giving toys to needy children and buying food for families, but that year she knew of a need very close to home.

Bev had a friend, a mom with two children who was diagnosed with cancer and had to be hospitalized. The timing couldn't have been worse. Bev knew how much mothers did at Christmas: they were the gift-buyers, gift-wrappers, and stocking stuffers.

That Christmas, Bev volunteered to do things for that family that a mom would have done. She told her children they could be her helpers, like elves helping Santa.

For weeks, she and her children sat on the kitchen floor wrapping presents for the Murphy children. Krissy kept thinking about how lonely her friend April must be without a mom. "Don't you think we should pray about April's mom?" she suggested. So they prayed and cried and wrapped.

That Christmas, Bev's children learned that giving sometimes involves heartache as well as joy, something the Father must have felt as He gave the gift of His Son.

_____

*May my children be drawn closer to God's heart as they learn more about giving this season.*

*We have seen His star in the East and have come to worship Him.*
—MATT. 2:2

Do you know how the legendary star of Bethlehem came to rest over the manger where Jesus was born? Charles Tazewell, in his story *The Littlest Angel,* offers one explanation.

The littlest angel, a rambunctious four-year-old, wonders what he should give the Christ child to celebrate His birth. Finally, it occurs to him that a child of God would treasure what he treasures. So he takes a rough wooden box that contains the things he loved most on earth—a butterfly he'd caught one day, a sky-blue bird's egg, two stones found by a river bank, his dog's old leather collar—and proudly places it at the throne of God.

But next to the glorious gifts of the other angels, his box looks ugly. He is ashamed. Then he hears the voice of God saying that of all the angels' gifts, the small box pleases Him the most, for it contains the things His Son will cherish when He lives on earth as a boy.

There is a breathless pause in heaven as the lowly gift is transformed into a radiant star, lighting up the whole night sky, and lighting the way for all men to find the greatest gift of all.

*A child's heart naturally blesses.*

*And a little child shall lead them.*
—ISA. 11:6

I believe my children had heavenly memories when they were very small," said one mother.

To some degree children have a natural capacity to bless. Not yet entangled in the muddle of daily living, they have a way of seeing into the heart of things and valuing what is most important. There is much they can teach us.

Jane still remembers the day she felt frazzled, stressed out, tired from Christmas shopping and trying to do so much for her family. She broke down and cried. "I'm tired of being a mother," she sobbed.

"Then be a daddy," said Jane's daughter.

"I'm afraid I can't do that."

"Then be a kid," said Jane's son.

So that's what Jane decided to do. She just let everything go and played all day.

Another mom was rescued from anxiety by her little one, who reminded her to give her worries to God. "When I go to bed," he said smiling, "I just give all my worries to God because He's going to be up all night anyway."

*Today I will learn what my children have to teach.*

*He blesses the home of the righteous.*
—PROV. 3:33 NIV

Learning to give and receive the blessing, that deep sense of love and acceptance we all long for, is a family affair, something we can work toward together. Children can remind a busy mom to slow down and value herself, a wife can affirm a husband with praise, a loving dad can show active commitment by taking a son fishing or a daughter on a special dinner date.

Home is not just a place to hang your hat. It is a laboratory for living, a place where we can learn to honor and serve one another in love. These words describe how a home can become a place of blessing.

> *Home is where you can be silent*
>   *and still be heard,*
>     *where you can ask*
>     *and find out who you are,*
>       *where people laugh with you*
>     *and about yourself,*
>       *where sorrow is divided*
>     *and joy multiplied*
>       *where we share, and love, and grow*
>           —AUTHOR UNKNOWN

*Lord, teach us as a family how to make our home a place of blessing.*

> *But those who plan what is good find love and faithfulness.*
> —PROV. 14:22 NIV

In order to reach a destination, you need to know where you are going. In the same way, in order to make a home a place of blessing, family members need to agree on the direction they are going and how they are going to get there. We have found it is helpful for families to set goals, even write up a family constitution to unite a home around certain fundamental principles.

As our children grew up, Norma and I (Gary) must have said thousands of times: "The two most important things in life are to honor God and to honor people." If the children dishonored someone, inside or outside the family, there was a sure and swift consequence.

Out of these two foundational principles, we established six basic family rules. Together they make up our family contract to which we have all agreed and signed.

Having a written set of objectives has greatly contributed to our family's peace, harmony and security. A family plan is essential if you want to consistently build the blessing into your loved ones' lives on a daily basis.

---

*Father, guide us as our family creates a plan that will offer clear direction for the future.*

*Now may the Lord direct your hearts into the love of God.*
—2 THESS. 3:5

A family plan gives us direction for building a loving home. It is just as important to seek God's direction in developing a common vision for how we can bless others outside the home. To formulate a family mission statement, you might ask questions like, "Where do we want to go as a family? What kind of family are we going to be? What is it, Lord, that You would like us to accomplish for You?"

Year ago, my (Gary's) family asked these questions. We prayed together, talked to other families, read widely, and grappled with principles in Scripture. We came to the conclusion that *the family* was the most important element in society, and we wanted to dedicate our family to enriching other families.

This is *our* mission. Another family's goal might be to raise money for a missionary project, or serve the poor in the inner city or get involved in neighborhood evangelism.

If you don't establish a clearly defined direction for your family, you will find other people or life's circumstances setting it for you.

God has a unique mission for your family. What can you do to define it and help it come about?

*Lord, what potential we have as a family! Show us how we can release it to serve You.*

> *They have forsaken Me, the fountain of living*
> *waters, and hewn themselves cisterns—broken*
> *cisterns that can hold no water.*
> —JER. 2:13

Parents know this scene well. Your child pleads for something new—something he wants more than anything in the world (right then!). You buy it for him. Within days (perhaps even the same day!), the desired object is discarded for lack of interest.

As adults, we do the same thing. In our seminars across the country, we give people a word picture that describes how we all try to satisfy our deep thirst for fulfillment with things that don't satisfy. In wanting to drink from the goodness of life, it is as if we throw a bucket into three wells, one marked "Others," another called "Locations," and still another labeled "Things."

We dip into relationships, thinking, maybe a relationship, an affair, a new friend will satisfy the emptiness we feel. Or maybe we think a new home, a new location, will bring fulfillment. Lastly, we try to fill that deep inner craving with things: more money, a new car, or a better job.

The more we try to get happiness from these things, the more disappointed we are. There is only one Well that can satisfy our need.

*Oh Lord, forgive me for looking for fulfillment in all the wrong places. Only Your love can fill my life to overflowing.*

*Delight yourself also in the LORD, and He shall give
you the desires of your heart.* —PS. 37:4

What are the desires of your heart? Probably some
are on the tip of your tongue. A happy home? A dream
fulfilled? Clear direction? A new beginning? Others
you might not be able to express so easily. God knows
our desires—spoken and unspoken.

He is the Source of all blessing. The Source of all joy.
A real and ever-renewable Source of life. Jesus is
called the Living Water. "Whoever drinks the water
that I shall give him will never thirst," He promises.
"But the water that I shall give him will become in him
a fountain of water springing up into everlasting life"
(John 4:14).

How can you continue to be filled by this unfailing
spring of refreshment? By being in the Word daily and
in prayer continually. By delighting in God's company.
By letting Him fill your life with good things, things
that will last.

Blessing will flow into your life as you draw refreshment from Him and let it flow out to others. And in
the midst of that gentle ebb and flow, you'll find a new
rhythm to living, a new hope, a new purpose, a new
energy.

———————

*Today is the first day of the rest of your life.*

# *Notes*

1. Taken from a sermon by Gary Klingsporn at Colonial Church, Edina, MN, January 10, 1993.
2. From Betsy Lee, *Miracle in the Making* (Minneapolis: Augsburg, 1983), 106. Used with permission.
3. Ibid, 22.
4. Margaret Therkelsen, *The Love Exchange* (Wilmore, KY: Bristol Books, 1990), 19.

# *About the Authors*

**G**ary Smalley, president of Today's Family, is a doctoral candidate in marriage and family counseling and has a master's degree from Bethel Seminary in St. Paul, Minnesota. His previous best-selling books include *If Only He Knew, For Better or Best, The Key to Your Child's Heart, Joy That Lasts,* and *The Gift of the Blessing.*

**J**ohn Trent is team teaching "Love Is a Decision" seminars with Gary Smalley and is doing seminars himself on "The Blessing" throughout the country. He is president of his own ministry, "Encouraging Words." John holds a Ph.D. in marriage and family counseling and has a master's degree from Dallas Theological Seminary. With Gary he wrote a number of books, including *The Language of Love, Love Is a Decision, The Two Sides of Love,* and *The Gift of the Blessing.* He lives in Phoenix with his wife, Cynthia, and daughters, Kari Lorraine and Laura Catherine.